THE ALASKA CHRONICLES

THE ALASKA CHRONICLES

by Miles Nolte

DEPARTURE

ISBN: 0-615-27632-6

Published in 2009 by Departure Publishing, LLC

Departure Publishing
P.O. Box 160818
Austin, TX 78716
(512) 347-8336

www.departurepublishing.com

Edited by Alison Tartt
Book design by Barbara Jezek
Photography, pages 96–120, by Miles Nolte
Jacket photography by Tosh Brown

Printed by Sheridan Books, Inc., Ann Arbor, MI
Printed on recycled paper

This book is for Mimi, who believed in it long before I did.

I also want to thank my parents, Tessa Andrews, Tosh Brown, Tom Bie, and of course the Alaska crew. Without all of you this never would have happened.

PUBLISHER'S NOTE

The original version of *The Alaska Chronicles* was posted as *The AK Chronicles* by Miles Nolte (screen name "Gaper") on *The Drake* magazine's Internet message board during the summer of 2007.

The Urban Dictionary defines a "gaper" as one who is generally found as an amazed onlooker when viewing any display of actual skill.

At the end of the season Miles' writings had attracted over 3,000 readers from Singapore to Germany.

The names of people and places have been changed. Any resemblance to persons living or dead is coincidental.

ARRIVAL

After thirteen hours of travel the dog and I have landed in the booming metropolis of King Salmon, Alaska. We began our trek yesterday in Montana, laid over in Seattle, and changed airlines in Anchorage, where we swapped the large jet for a battered twin-prop with no headroom or beverage service. Lehua, my three-year-old golden retriever, absolutely hates flying. At the Anchorage baggage claim she burst from her kennel when I cracked the gate and began howling and whining, running between my legs, and jamming her snout into my crotch. It took two gate agents and me to get her back into the crate for the final leg.

I'm back. I've returned, against my better judgment, for another summer of guiding. I've arrived with soft, indoor hands for another season of massive trout, eighteen-hour workdays, skidding jet boats, and wilderness isolation. From now through September I'll be living in a glorified tent, detangling knots, and fluffing the egos of anglers whose weekly expense reports exceed my annual income. Having walked out on yet another relationship, I'm facing four months with this furry, hyperactive blond as my only female companion. Her oily coat and my scraggly beard smell like grime and recycled cabin air.

Outside the sagging, corrugated airport terminal I find

a loitering collection of gaunt commercial fishermen and scruffy, tired-eyed young men carrying rod tubes and dry bags, guys like me, fishing guides. The biting flies immediately swarm my face, and I realize after a quick scan of the potholed parking lot that there's no one here to meet me. There's no rust-eaten, off-white Suburban with keys in the ignition, as promised. Ken, my boss, has either forgotten about me, or he's running late. Either way, I'm not especially surprised. Welcome back, Miles.

The town of King Salmon, population 442, sits on the north bank of the Naknek River, roughly 300 miles southwest of Anchorage. The town consists of a grocery, two bars, a Wells Fargo bank, a marine supply store, a boatyard, a few airfreight services, a small army of bush pilots, and one hotel. There used to be two hotels but the Quinnat Landing burned to the ground last summer. Lucky for us, the King Ko Inn is still standing, so we are not without a watering hole.

There are fourteen miles of roadway connecting King Salmon to Naknek, where its namesake river empties into Bristol Bay. Naknek is a similarly squat but slightly more depressing town with several canneries and a large commercial fishing fleet. Weathered houses line the streets and riverbanks, and mongrel dogs roam in loose packs.

Luckily, I will spend little time in either town. Instead of drunken cannery workers and cynical natives, I'll spend my summer contending with 800-pound brown bears and wealthy, rotund white men. The lodge I'll be working for is located on an uninhabited river that drains into Bristol Bay. There are no roads through the desolate bog and tundra between town and the lodge, so our travels require a pounding boat ride across the bay and a long, winding run upriver.

I'm in the process of deciding my next move (hitch a ride or go to the bar?) when the weathered Suburban pulls up with our lodge logo peeling off the back window. I was hoping that Ken might escort me to the house he keeps in town for a little rest, and maybe some food. I should have known better: that would have set the wrong precedent for the coming season.

Thirty minutes after my plane lands, I find myself hanging off the back of a tractor and scavenging a 500-gallon fuel tank out of a ravine. From what I could gather, the property and the fuel tank belonged to a local who had run short of funds during his spring bender. My boss had found him languishing in the bar, so they swapped a couple of hundreds and now we have a new fuel tank. A while later, after I had been gratefully deposited at the house, the boss went back to the King Ko and found that the entire payment for the fuel tank had turned into whiskey. After another session of Let's Make a Deal, the native parted with a second fuel tank—that one still half full of diesel.

Back at the house, I'm stuck alone with one of the new guides, Dan. He arrived a day before I did, and he appears totally taken aback by his new surroundings. He seems like a nice enough kid, but the whole experience of the first day has him wired into a fit of nonstop chatter. In the few hours that I've spent with him, I've learned that he already knows everything about anything. That's a tough spot to be in at age twenty; where will he go from there?

After an hour of his ceaseless yammering, I've excused myself and picked out a bunk with heavy, dirty sheets. The dog has been banished to the shed, where she will spend one last night in grumpy confinement before she arrives at the lodge for a summer of unfettered canine bliss.

I've plugged in my laptop to charge and I've begun piecing together scraps and thoughts that I can hopefully weave into a narrative of the coming summer. I don't exactly have a plan for this writing, but I do know from last year's experience that there will be stories worth recounting. My hope is to use this project as a confidant, a reservoir into which I can pour all of my triumphs and misgivings. Maybe if I write it all down it will help me understand exactly why I keep signing up for this. The pay is decent as long as you don't work it out to an hourly wage.

I'm weary and travel worn but my mind is buzzing. Excitement and dread are roiling in my stomach. I know what lies ahead of me in the coming months and it all starts tomorrow.

Scratch that—it's already begun.

SPRING RIVER

We missed the morning high tide. I guess staying out late bartering for used equipment took its toll on the boss.

The ebb and flow of seawater dictates everything we do in the preseason. At low tide there's not enough water at the mouth of the river to get boats (even jet boats) in or out. Around here, there are two high and two low tides in each twenty-four-hour period, and they can fluctuate by more than twenty-five feet. All of our goods have to be transported from town to camp by boat, so the tides set the schedules. If you miss one, you have ten to thirteen hours until the next.

I got to sleep until 9:00 a.m. That's a luxury that I doubt I'll see again for quite some time. We puttered around the house and then went to town, running errands and killing time until there was enough water to make the crossing. On our way to the boat ramp we swung by the grocery and I picked up some essentials. Beer, whiskey, and porn are all absolute necessities when spending four months in a remote camp full of men. The proprietors of all local establishments know this, and the prices reflect my desperation and their monopoly. Twenty bucks for a twelve-pack of Oly (in cans), thirty-five for a bottle of Wild Turkey, and twenty-five for a copy of Chic magazine.

We finally launched on the evening tide at 8:00 p.m. There are more hours of sunlight than darkness at this time of year, so we still had plenty of light for the long run to camp. Crossing Bristol Bay is not the scenic Alaskan journey one might imagine. It's a wide expanse of muddy, cold, brackish water lined with the skeletal remains of abandoned canneries, rotting edifice corpses that would make a perfect backdrop for a low-budget horror movie. The lower part of our river isn't much nicer. Late May is considered early spring in Alaska: the growing-season moisture is still locked in the frozen tundra, so the foliage remains brown and lifeless.

Two hours after leaving the ramp in Naknek, Ken, Dan and I entered the upper river, where the water cleared and the landscape changed. There the river transforms from a wide, muddy crawl through coastal tundra into a beautiful freestone flow pocked with scrub islands and emergent gravel bars. Stands of pine and spruce dot the shores and rolling hillsides.

As we ran upriver, I drank in the familiarity of the water I will call home until September and noted the changes in landscape carved by the ice floes of early spring. Trees fall into the current, run aground in mid-river, and whole gravel bars rise and fall. The entire character of a stretch of water can change from one season to the next.

In the bright twilight the roar of our Chevy 350 inboard jet spooked a cow moose so pregnant she could barely scamper away on her spindly legs. A lone grizzly, young and emaciated, ambled off when we startled him from his lean-season scavenging. River otters, beavers, and eagles dove, scurried, and swooped as we pushed upriver toward camp. The low, early-season river flows make navigating the narrow channels a bit challenging, but we made it through the braids, lightly grazing only a few gravel bars.

At 11:00 p.m. the boat wake lapped the edge of the lodge dock, and two gangly yellow labs came bounding down the plank walkway. Lehua all but flung herself out of the boat to greet her summertime companions. The dogs were followed by a trail of familiar faces: Josh, Dick, Paul, and Tim had all returned for another season and met us at the dock with weary grins. Mixed in were two faces new to me—Mitch, who had been the head guide for many years but was returning after a multi-year hiatus, and Nick, a new guide around my age who came to us from a lodge on the Goodnews River. I cleated off the boat and exchanged firm handshakes and masculine hugs (the kind that involve repeated back-patting) with my friends. I haven't seen or spoken to these guys in months, but the passing of time hasn't faded the bond—a brotherhood forged with toil and interdependence.

The evening sky was still dimly lit as we unloaded the boat. Even though the sun will eventually set today, we'll reach a point during mid-summer when it will barely touch the horizon before lifting off again.

After peeling off my waders and eating a cold hamburger, I adjourned to one of the guest cabins, again with Dan, the jabbering rookie. When he launched into a spirited pronouncement of his father's extraordinary fly-tying talents, I put on my headphones and cranked up my iPod to drown out his voice and establish a rhythm with my laptop keyboard.

MAY 24

ADRIFT

I awoke at 5:00 a.m. with my ears still ringing from last night's jet boat ride. Another supply run was scheduled and we needed to catch the morning tide.

I took the helm of a twenty-two-foot aluminum v-hull with a 350 inboard jet. I hadn't driven a boat since the previous summer, and there I was piloting one of our largest crafts through the skinny, early-season channels. It was cold on the river and I was feeling groggy. When I took the wrong lane around a sunken tree, I overcorrected on the wheel and nearly spun out. After that moment of awakening I backed off on the throttle and continued downriver, sipping my coffee with trembling hands.

About thirty miles down from camp, the engine began to sputter. It had been faltering and gagging for an hour or so, dropping power and threatening to fall off plane before surging back to life. As I fell further behind the group, Josh, a good friend who is no stranger to boats (or boat failures), turned around and pulled alongside to see if I was okay. I told him the problem and he shrugged his shoulders. There was a tide to catch and Ken was already well ahead. I told him to go on without me—I'd get there if I could. He said if I didn't make it, he'd come back for me later in the day.

Soon after he roared away, the engine finally coughed and fell silent. I was left drifting in the muddy slack of tidewater. If the weather held, they would be back for me before nightfall. If the winds picked up too much more, they would shack up in King Salmon and I'd be left to fend for myself during the night. That's the way it goes here. Preparing for the season is our priority. Unless you're in immediate danger when your boat dies, your only choice is to wait for the next one to come along. Last year Josh spent fourteen hours on a beach under a tarp when the boat he was driving conked out. He later confessed it was one of the best days he'd had all season: he had nothing to do but catch up on his sleep.

For the next six hours I sat in the boat and watched the waning tide. Occasionally I would pull up the anchor and move it farther offshore to keep the boat from settling aground as the water level decreased beneath the hull. I passed the time tinkering with the engine, reading a book, and sleeping under a tarp of my own. Beyond that, there wasn't much to do. Looking back, I would have to agree with Josh: it wasn't such a bad day.

By 2:00 p.m. the wind was etching white-capped ridges into the blank canvas of the muddy bay. Guessing that they probably wouldn't try the crossing in these conditions, I sat and mulled over my options. I could stay there and wait for them to make it back (maybe tomorrow morning) or try to nurse the boat back upstream to camp. Neither option was particularly attractive, but the proactive move seemed better at the time.

After a few more tries the engine finally cranked, but it still wasn't running at full power. I started limping back upriver, hoping it wouldn't cut out at an inopportune moment. I was making decent progress and feeling pretty good about my situation until I realized that I didn't have enough gas to make it all the way back to camp. The plan had been to refuel in Naknek but I didn't make it that far. Approximately eight miles upriver from where I had been stranded sits the largest lodge on the river. It's a long haul downriver from our camp, so we don't see them often. They run a large staff, though, so I figured there would be people there and, more important, fuel. Last year we bailed out their head guide when his tanks ran dry up near our location. I figured they owed us one.

As I docked my boat in their slough, I noticed a plane had just landed on their airstrip. It was a de Havilland Otter, one of the largest planes used in this area, and it was birthing a collection of wide-eyed rookie guides fresh from Anchorage. I had heard a rumor that this lodge had been sold and the new owner, in an effort to cut costs, had laid off the majority of the senior guides. He had replaced them with a crew of cheaper greenies whose mean age looked to be about nineteen. A burly, white-haired man with an impressive mustache heard my clattering approach and broke off from his group of new recruits. He intercepted me as I walked up from the slough. He didn't return my smile but shook my hand and agreed to give me enough gas to get back upriver.

While I was at the dock waiting for their maintenance guy to arrive and fuel my boat, I heard the drone of the cavalry approaching in the distance. My fearless compatriots came raging up the slough, figuring I had probably made my way here since they couldn't find me downriver. I had been guided by the old mariner's adage "Any port in a storm," but my friends had braved a low tide and six-foot waves on their trip across Bristol Bay.

I waved off the maintenance guy with thanks and siphoned a share of gas from one of our other boats. The motor started back up easily but quit again after a couple of miles. Our only choice was to ditch the cripple in a sheltered eddy. We'll tow it back to King Salmon for repairs on our next trip downriver.

After sixteen unproductive hours in a derelict boat, I finally made it back to camp, stuffed my face, and crawled into bed. Even Dan's relentless vocal spewing won't keep me from falling asleep tonight.

MAY 26

UNSKILLED LABOR

Building in the rain and boating to and from town is about all we'll do until the clients arrive on June 7. For the past two days we've been working on the wooden platforms that support the guide housing (Weatherport tents). Muddy boots and rubber rain jackets are the choice apparel for our construction crew. I look the part but lack the skills to hang with the other guys. Mitch, the loud and gregarious head guide, has built his life with his hands—most of these guys have. I grew up in a house where the only tools Dad owned were Sears brand, and anytime they appeared we knew that copious swearing and a visit from some professional (plumber, electrician, carpenter) would soon follow.

I spent a summer after college working as a carpenter's apprentice: hauling lumber, making cuts, and painting. I worked hard and did what I was told so he kept me around, but I was never much good at any of it except the hauling. I would spend hours painting a bathroom, trying to be meticulous and clean. When I was done, the carpenter would walk through and shake his head, wondering aloud how a bright kid could fuck up a single coat of paint. I'd always respond the same way: "Just talented, I guess."

I tried hard to help the guys assemble the platforms, falling into the few routines I knew. I asked them the length of boards, made the cuts, and fetched the tools they needed. I felt perpetually underfoot, muddling simple tasks and slowing everyone down. Like a child trying to help his dad with an elaborate garage project, I was eventually accepted by the group as an inevitable hindrance to the process.

At mealtime, though, I'm a bit more useful. Our early-season cupboards are limited and the chef won't arrive until just before the clients. Until he gets here, we're responsible for our cooking, and I know my way around a kitchen better than a jobsite. I still feel somewhat emasculated when preparing meals for the group, but at least I'm making a positive contribution.

The biggest problem that I'm facing right now is my lack of gear. I packed only a small overnight bag for my first run upriver from King Salmon because I planned to return the next morning for the rest of my belongings. Getting stuck with a dead boat prevented me from picking up my stuff, and things were so scattered and chaotic in King Salmon that the guys forgot to bring any of my gear back with them on the supply run.

I have no clean clothes, no fishing gear (not that I have any time to fish), no pillow, and no sheets—and I won't be able to get any of it for at least four more days when the next supply run is scheduled. Fortunately, I do have my Xtratufs, the sturdy rubber boots that are a mainstay in this part of the country. And I also have my work gloves and a rain jacket. My clothes might be filthy, but at least I can stay dry while getting in everyone's way.

As soon as my platform is complete I'll be able to erect

my private (Weatherport) living quarters. Until then I'm still bunking with Dan, who continues to talk unabated. I have not wet a line, my clothes smell like ass, and it hasn't stopped raining since I got here. I am coming to the conclusion that I might be a masochist for returning to work here another season.

UNSKILLED LABOR, PART II

I am a fishing guide, not a carpenter. This fact, while apparent every day, was excruciatingly obvious today.

We spent the morning assembling and erecting our communal quarters for eating and relaxing. It's a large round tent with a clear Plexiglas nipple on top—a yurt, to be exact. Our yurt is made with a synthetic shell, unlike the wool felt used by the Mongolians who originated the design. Despite our propensity for producing funk, I'm guessing that ours might still be less pungent than the Mongolian model. An engineering degree would be recommended for the erection of this structure, and since we are all fishing guides . . . well, you get the picture. And if the project itself wasn't difficult enough, the steady 20 mph wind added an extra element of frustration.

Eventually we worked out a system whereby Paul stood on a stepladder set atop a picnic table. With one hand he held aloft a wooden ring with slots cut in it. With the other hand he slid fifteen-foot two-by-fours into the slots in the ring. This apparatus would eventually form the roof apex with the beams radiating out from the ring like wheel spokes. From there, the opposite ends of the beams were attached to ten-foot vertical studs spaced about three feet apart and supported at the base with metal brackets screwed to the floor platform.

The theory here is that once you get enough wood applying opposite pressure, it creates structural stability. Until that stability is achieved, you simply have lots of heavy beams placed precariously at high altitudes. When one of them falls, it's likely to inflict pain. That was confirmed when a beam slipped from its slot and came down on me like a sprung bear trap. It smashed me on the shoulder, and I crumpled to the floor of the unfinished yurt, writhing and moaning in the manliest voice I could muster while trying not to look too much like the skinny kid who took a dodge ball in the solar plexus during recess. A few inches to the left and I would have taken it right on the noggin. I doubt that my paint-stained cap would have offered much protection.

After the yurt incident I spent the remainder of the day building a table. Now, I realize that anyone with a modicum of carpentry skills wouldn't require an entire afternoon to build one table, but along with my ingrained inability to build anything, including Lincoln Log structures as a kid, you must also consider the source of materials. The plywood that I was using had been lying on the tundra since last summer, where it had suffered through Alaska's brutal winter freeze and spring thaw cycle. Conditions such as those cause plywood to warp like a question mark. Also, this table was to be mounted against a curved wall, and I had nothing but a circular saw to make my cuts.

It won't win any woodworking prizes, but it stands up against gravity and you can even rest small things on top of it. For me, that's an achievement.

MAY 28

A BREAK IN THE WEATHER

I awoke today to a strange auditory void, the startling absence of a particular sound that has greeted me every morning since I arrived in camp. As usual I was rattled awake by Dick, the camp manager, yelling outside my window. "It's eight o'clock. Get your asses up!"

This morning, however, as I lay in bed trying to clear the cobwebs, I didn't hear the usual timbre of pattering raindrops on the tin roof. When I looked outside, there were scattered clouds and a bright object that looked suspiciously like the sun.

Dick was outside the cabin when I opened the door. "What the fuck you doing in there, beating off?"

"Yeah, we were just finishing. Dan's still in there if you're feeling frisky."

"That fucking kid is useless," he growled, with enough volume to be heard through the open door.

Dick is a surly bastard in his early sixties. He's solidly built with sinewy arms and a thick, black beard flecked with gray. His intolerance for laziness is justified by the fact that he works longer and harder than most of the people in camp despite being twice their age. An electrician for thirty years, he supplemented his income by guiding. After retirement he started guiding full time in the summers, moving between remote Alaska and his home in upstate New York.

The stories of his youth are carved into the deep crevices of his tanned neck, and when he tells them he usually begins with "Back when I was drinking . . ." He has a few stock anecdotes that he likes to tell repeatedly. One of my favorites usually comes out when he's griping about Ken's children scattering their toys around the lodge.

"When I was a kid, we were too poor to buy toys. I just cut holes in my pockets and played with myself."

After spouting one of his little yarns, he'll usually pull an orange plastic whistle from his pocket and blow a sharp, piercing blast. "The bullshit whistle" he calls it. The whistle also appears when someone is visibly annoyed or deep into an extended session of bitching. When he blows the whistle, his aged face takes on the look of a child pulling a defiant prank on a self-righteous adult. And, as you might guess, the timing of the bullshit whistle often inflames an already tense situation.

Last year, after a particularly inopportune whistle-blowing incident, I turned to him and said, "If you blow that god-damn whistle one more time I swear I'm going to jam it down your throat." He gave me his trademark grin and then blew with all his might. I tackled him to the ground and began trying to wrestle the offending bit of molded plastic from his meaty fist. Despite my being thirty-five years his junior, I couldn't pry it free from his grip and after a few minutes I collapsed to the side, rolling on the ground and laughing in an effort to disguise the embarrassment of getting manhandled by a grandfather of six.

He guides only a handful of days a season now, spending his time instead walking around camp, picking up errant tools, muttering angrily to himself, and riding the young guys like rented mules. His gruffness is offset by the tenderness he shows to Ken's young kids, who refer to him as "Uncle Dick" and invade his lap regularly during dinner. He threatens to quit at least twice a season. When asked where to put a tool or how to fix a boat while he's in a foul mood, he usually answers, "I don't know, burn the fucker."

After breakfast we went back to work on the guide housing under sunny skies and pleasant temperatures. This year the unwashed help has been moved farther up the hill from where the clients sleep. This may have something to do with our consistent urinating from the doorsteps of our Weatherports. Or perhaps the final straw was last year's drunken bet on who could sing the best "Eye of the Tiger" at 3:00 a.m. Come on, now: who can't appreciate being woken in the middle of the night by inebriated fishing guides singing Survivor?

I didn't win.

Around 10:00 a.m. we got a call from town that the boss was on his way across the bay. This season we have two new toys, and both of them have been sitting in town waiting for the river to rise enough to allow safe passage through the braids. Toy No. 1 is a brand new tractor that we'll use to construct a landing strip on top of the hill. Of course, if you buy a tractor, you'll need the means of hauling it upriver to camp. Toy No. 2 is a 28-foot dual 350 inboard jet with a drop gate on the front—a monstrosity of a jet boat, custom built for our operation.

Even though the river is still a bit low for transporting heavy equipment by boat, Ken just can't stand the idea of that brand new tractor sitting idle in town. If he were to wait a few days, there would probably be plenty of water in the river and less reason to worry about piling up expensive equipment on a gravel bar. Patience, however, is not Ken's strongest attribute; getting shit done is.

At 3:30 p.m. we heard the roar of the engines blasting upriver. Ten minutes later Ken barreled into the boat slough at the helm of his new diamond-plate landing craft. Grinning madly, he dropped the gate and we unloaded our new bright orange assault vehicle that we'll use to storm the tundra and force the earth to bend at our mercy. Along with the tractor he was carrying all the gear and clothing I'd been missing, plus the beer I left in town. I'm not sure I've ever been happier to see my boss. At that moment he was a fairy godmother in saggy neoprene waders driving a v-hull aluminum chariot from hell.

In the evening, I skipped out on dishes and snuck away to fish for an hour. The weather was perfect: cool with scattered clouds and hardly a breath of wind. Lehua and I walked a half mile upstream from camp, squishing through the thawing tundra and fording a few small springs. We stopped on a mid-river gravel bar with a deep, slow trough against the bank where the trout like to hold early in the season. The cork felt good in my hand as I fell into the rhythm of casting. The fish were active, hungry from the spawn, and unwary after months of solitude. In an hour of fishing I hooked four and landed one deeply colored rainbow. One of the fish that jumped off was an absolute hog of at least twenty-seven inches. When the light finally faded into the stark and extended dusk, I called the dog and we trudged back to the lodge. My body was sore but my spirits were high. Fishing is something I know how to do, an activity that fortifies my self-confidence.

Once again I'm now holed up in my cabin, trying to ignore the inane drivel of my temporary roommate. God, I can't wait for those Weatherports to be finished. In the sanctuary of my headphones, I reflect on a truly magnificent day: we got the boat to camp, we got our houses halfway built, and I even got to fish. That's more than I dared to ask for.

JUNE 2

TOWN SUCKS

I spent the past three days in town without shoes, pants, or a toothbrush. I can adamantly say that I wish to spend no more time there.

On Thursday (I think it was Thursday—my concept of days has receded to a vague outline) I awoke to the news that I would accompany our fearless leader across the bay on the morning high tide. I jumped on board for the day's mission, but Ken neglected to tell me that I would be staying in town for a stretch and spelling Dillis, who had been there for several days. In addition to patience, communication is another one of Ken's weak points.

As a result of this omission, I was grossly unprepared. I left the camp wearing waders and boots, but those aren't really my preferred attire in which to work, drive, and eat for three days. Luckily I found a pair of Ken's Top-Siders at the house that I could squeeze my feet into and a pair of his sweatpants that would fit two of me. I purchased a pair of overpriced boxers at the mercantile. I was happy to pay triple the going rate to avoid borrowing another man's skivvies.

Back in April we sent several shipping containers from Seattle with most of our supplies for the season. Retrieving this glut of essentials is the reason we've been making daily runs to town with the new landing craft. The containers left Seattle with 15,000 pounds of lumber, the new tractor (complete with a backhoe, auger, box blade, and brush box), four new sixteen-foot skiffs, nine new Weatherport tents, $4,000 worth of new power tools, and the bounty of a $7,000 Costco run. You should have seen the looks we got as we corralled thirty-five of their big, flat, orange carts and stacked them with our haul.

With the shipping containers stored in Naknek, one of us has to be in town to unload materials from the container and truck them to the ramp for loading when the landing craft arrives.

Beyond the actual loading and transfer of supplies, daily life in town goes something like this: The phone typically starts ringing at 4:00 a.m. because people on the East Coast either don't realize where we are or they don't understand time zones. At 7:00 a.m. I begin answering and returning the flood of calls from booked clients, prospective clients, telemarketers, the occasional wrong number, my boss on his sat-phone, and his wife trying to figure out where the hell he is.

By 9:00 a.m. I'm on my way to the shipping containers to fill the van with supplies and whatever else the boss has asked me to purchase in town. Sometime around 2:00 p.m. the boat arrives and we scramble to get it loaded before the tide starts to recede. From there we motor to the gas docks to refuel the boat for the return trip. That part is actually kind of fun. The fueling station sits on a high dock with long, narrow metal ladders reaching down to the water. Depending on the tide, you might have to climb fifty to sixty feet on the swaying rusted bars.

By 5:00 p.m. I'm exhausted and heading to the bar where I'll spend far more money than I've earned during the course of the day. Suffering in the dearth of estrogen, I jabber into the night with scraggly commercial fishermen, cannery workers from various countries, and surly natives. There are usually somewhat attractive women working behind the bar—not local girls, but imports looking for a summer job and a little adventure. These are women with soft skin and sharp tongues; not classically beautiful and slightly flawed (narrow eyes, a crooked nose, bad teeth), but properly insulated with sufficient youth. They are worshipped openly and tipped handsomely on a nightly basis. They'd be considered average in my mid-size hometown, but here they are goddesses and they know it.

I try to be subtle and elusive while seeking the exact same thing that every other man in the bar wants. Just like them, I typically end up staying too late and drinking too much. Lonely, melancholy, and profoundly intoxicated, I spend the last of my cash on cab fare and return to the house just about the time the phone starts ringing.

Like I said, town sucks.

JUNE 4

HOME SWEET TENT

I'm glad to be back in camp. I'm glad to be working ten to thirteen hours a day carrying lumber, building walkways, fixing boats, and painting cabins. Okay, that last one is a lie. I hate painting, but I really don't mind the rest of it.

I finish my days sore and ready for sleep, and then I wake up still tired—but at least I'm not hung over and broke and reeking of stale smoke and failure. Today I've got a freshly bandaged thumb, but it's a worthy trade-off because my Weatherport is finally complete. Yes, my coated canvas palace on the hill is now standing erect, and I'm looking forward to sleeping in my new bed and not sharing a room for the rest of the summer. Actually, "bed" might be a slight misrepresentation of what I'll be sleeping on. It's a plywood platform balanced atop uneven scraps of two-by-fours, with a foam pad, a sheet, and a pillow. My down sleeping bag provides warmth on colder nights. Despite what it lacks in traditional comfort, it's firm beneath my back and I have had no trouble sleeping on it.

The bloody thumb happened as I was stretching the walls of my tent and screwing them into the wooden floor. If the wall material is not flush against the wood, a continual stream of biting insects will pour into the room. Stretching a heavy canvas cover and holding it in place while trying to get a screw to bite into the wood beneath is a difficult task. Ideally, one would have three arms for this job. I've managed to get the cover tight by pushing my shoulder into it, while holding the screw in place with my left hand and using my right hand to operate the screw gun. On the last screw of the last wall, the Phillips bit slipped and plunged into the quick of my left thumb. I removed the metal piece from my flesh, and the cavern left behind immediately pooled with blood. I now know why some cultures use the fingernails as areas of interest during torture sessions. That shit hurts.

This year, my hands are returning earlier than normal to their condition of abused magnificence. Flecked with paint and traced with fissures of grime, they're beginning to resemble the cracked and strong instruments of labor that they became over the course of last season. The bandage will make knot-tying somewhat interesting. I'm hoping my thumb will heal before the first sports arrive in three days, but the pain and throbbing are telling me different.

It looks like this episode has just been interrupted by the roar of the approaching landing craft. As I lie here on my foam pad communing with my keyboard, I can hear the inevitable growl as it rolls upriver with a load of gas and lumber that must be unloaded tonight.

It's 11:42 p.m. I can't wait to start guiding.

JUNE 5

FUEL CRISIS

Three more days until the season opener and we continue to run
boatloads of supplies from town like drug smugglers with second
mortgages. We all resemble extras from the original *Night of the
Living Dead:* dirty, bedraggled, wild-eyed—but we're still on schedule to have most of our legwork done before the clients arrive.

This is a massive improvement from last season, when
we were still building a house for the boss and his family during
the bug-infested perpetual daylight of mid-July. After guiding for
a full day on the river, we would build for another eight hours or
until we were too tired to swing a hammer.

I won't pretend that I was the most effective or enthusiastic guide during those weeks, but the late-night toil of that first
season bonded me to the camp and my fellow guides. We worked
side by side with bent backs and aching legs. Walls were erected
in the haste of exhaustion, and when they strayed from the chalk
line in the wee hours of the morning, there were thrown tools and
shouts of frustration that would eventually turn into hysterical
laughter. It wasn't fun, but finishing that house became a matter of
pride. It forced me to harden, to bear down and reset my suburban,
college-instructor, 8-to-5 internal clock to a primal rhythm driven
by necessity. We did what needed to be done because there was no

other choice. There were no time clocks, just a pile of lumber that needed to be transformed into a two-story shelter. The more work we did, the sooner we would finish, and those late-night beers were the ones we looked forward to most.

Besides the housing project, there were other problems that threw last year's daily schedule into disarray. Last July a fuel barge pulled into the lower river, stopping about fifty miles downstream from us. Ken had ordered 1,600 gallons of gas from the barge. It was supposed to arrive in early June, but bad weather and a late spring delayed the arrival for over a month. Each day during that month we came back from guiding wondering if we would be called into service to fetch the fuel.

When the barge finally did arrive, it stayed for only twenty-four hours before moving on to the next drainage, which didn't leave us much time to transfer our gas. Most of the other lodges on the river are located near the mouth, so they had no trouble retrieving their shares. We had a much greater distance to travel, so that narrow window of time, combined with the large volume of fuel, made for a logistical nightmare.

I remember coming back from guiding the day that the barge arrived. I was at the dock unloading my clients when Ken came down the planked walkway. I could see from the determination in his shuffling gate that something was up. He is not a man who walks with purpose unless he truly has one. I was one of the first guides back that day, so I parked my small skiff and traded it for a larger vessel that was ready to go. It had a 90 hp outboard and a center steering console; all other nonessential gear had been removed. In the middle of the boat sat a large empty storage tank; it was one of those opaque plastic models encased in an aluminum cage. With its weight capacity, the craft couldn't handle a full load of gas, so I'd only be able to fill about a third of the storage tank.

I had never been at the helm of that boat, but my instructions from Ken were simple: get down to the barge as fast as possible, fill up with as much gas as the boat could haul, and then return to camp. The process would be repeated until the job was done. Every boat in the fleet would be running back and forth until all the fuel was safely stored at camp.

I'd been guiding for only a month and a half and I'd never driven a boat more than a few miles downstream. I was pretty sure that I knew the channels to avoid, but they were not yet ingrained in my memory. This would be trial by fire.

As I backed the boat out of the slough, radiating as much confidence as I could muster, Paul, who would be coming behind me in another boat, yelled from the dock, "You ever driven that boat before?"

"No."

"Miles, be careful. She slides—especially when she's empty. She slides."

"Okay."

"No, really. She slides."

"Got it."

"When you see the fuel barge, it's gonna be at the far end of a big island. It looks like you want to take the right channel, but you don't. Take the left channel."

"Okay."

As I pulled into the main channel and prepared to gun the throttle and bring the boat on step, Paul cupped his hands to his mouth and yelled at me again from the weathered cedar dock.

"SHE SLIDES!"

I could barely hear him over the roar of the engine as it thrust the bow skyward, but I knew what he said.

At first I drove cautiously, trying to get a feel for the center-console steering and the powerful engine. Paul was right; she did want to slide, and I could feel the hull trying to dart off course as I skidded through the turns. There's no rudder on a jet boat, so the only way to steer is to point it in the appropriate direction and give it gas. Without throttle there is no change in heading. You can spin the steering wheel all you want, but if you're not giving it power, you'll continue to go in the direction you were already traveling. If there's a rock, a tree, a gravel bar (or a bear) in your way, you cannot decelerate to avoid it; you can only maintain or increase your speed. These boats require a delicate touch. If you crank too sharply on the wheel, you'll spin out. Overcorrecting is not an option—at least not an attractive one.

I made three fuel runs down and back that night. Loaded with gas and driving upstream against the current was easy because the boat handled like she was running on rails. But with empty fuel tanks and the current pushing on my transom, the downstream runs were a bit dicey. By the second trip downriver I had gained some confidence. I knew where to go, and the steering felt good, so I gave her some juice and raced toward the barge with a mad, purposeful grin.

When I came to a narrow channel between a shallow bar on the port and a large boulder on the starboard side, I tried to take the line close to the bar to avoid the rock. When I saw that the water along the bar was skinnier than I had expected, I attempted a slight starboard correction. It seemed like a delicate turn of the wheel, but I was going too fast and the boat started to slide sideways straight for the boulder. I tried to steer back toward the channel but my momentum kept the stern of the boat aimed squarely at the boulder. At this point all I could do to keep the engine from smashing the rock was steer straight for it and push the throttle handle as far down as it would go. I was hoping that would swing the ass end of the boat back out and away from the imminent collision. Somehow it worked. I didn't look back, but I don't think I missed that slab of immovable earth by more than three inches. My hands were shaking badly, so I slowed it down until I reached the barge.

At 2:00 a.m., on my third and last trip upriver, I was driving through the braids in the dark and hoping that I wouldn't plant the boat on a gravel bar. I did hit one but was able to extricate the boat without any assistance, so that doesn't really qualify. I had loaded the opaque plastic storage tank a little heavier on that last trip, trying to haul as much fuel as possible back upriver so we could call it a night. What I failed to consider in my state of adrenalized exhaustion was how the extra weight would affect my fuel consumption.

Three miles from camp, the engine started to sputter. I pulled over to a mid-river island and checked the red, fifteen-gallon removable tank that fed the engine. It was dry. When I tried to refill it, I discovered another minor problem: even with the little red tank placed right next to the big storage tank, my siphon hose was not long enough to transfer the fuel. The hose dangled uselessly, well above the sloshing line in the storage tank. Despite my hundred-plus gallons of gas, I was dry where it counted.

As I worked with a wrench to unhook the bilge pump hose and splice it to my siphon (thus giving me enough length to reach the fuel), it occurred to me that I should keep an eye out for bears. That turned out to be a solid premonition. When I looked up and scanned my surroundings in the fading twilight, I found the outline of a large, fuzzy head swimming across the river directly toward my island. I had no shotgun in the boat or bear deterrent of any kind. As the surging adrenaline quickly purged the fatigue from my system, I began yelling at the bear and banging the wrench on the hull of the aluminum boat. Bears generally don't like loud noises, and for some reason they're especially displeased with the sound of metal hitting metal. He changed direction slightly but still swam to the island where I was stranded and hurriedly disappeared into the chest-high grass.

For the next forty-five minutes I stood my ground, yelled myself hoarse, and banged on the boat until my hand went numb from the metallic vibration. Utterly preoccupied with the bear, I ceased doing anything productive to get myself out of the stranded-with-no-fuel situation. The bear never made any aggressive moves toward me. In fact, I never saw the bear again, but that didn't keep me from imagining his ghostly rustling through the windswept foliage next to my boat.

Sometime after 3:00 a.m., a dark figure motored alongside that was shrouded in a camouflage jumpsuit with his hood cinched tight against the biting wind. It was Ken, and he found me standing on the bow of my stranded boat, still grasping the wrench and panting heavily from a combination of fear and physical exertion. He looked at me for a moment and then asked me a perfectly logical question.

"What the fuck are you doing?"

I told him about the bear and he glanced around in the dark, skeptically, before handing me a full five-gallon tank and a few comments about my choice of a weapon.

I still get an occasional ration of shit for that episode, and admittedly I could have handled the situation differently. I should have just worked on getting my fuel transferred once I saw the bear startle. Experience with the bears up here has taught me that they have very little interest in crossing paths with humans. Coastal brown bears in this area are mainly focused on consuming a sufficient number of calories to survive the winter and avoiding large-caliber slugs during hunting season. Negative interactions with people do not further either of these goals. That said, I'd still rather not find myself alone, again, on a mid-river island in the wee hours of the morning with a curious bear.

JUNE 8

OPENING DAY

Today was our first day of guiding clients, and as you might expect, it began as an absolute clusterfuck.

Most of the guests' luggage didn't make the flight from Anchorage to King Salmon, so everyone was scrambling about and trying to find waders, jackets, fleeces, and equipment. The guides were bickering about who was going where and which boat would be taken by whom. Weeks of pent-up frustration among the staff was finally coming to a head.

Being the lowest-ranking guide taking clients today, I wound up getting switched out of my boat at the last minute. I scrambled to put together seats, PFDs, flares—all of the essential items that I had already organized into a boat that was taken from me when someone else pulled rank. I was briefly pissed but chose to let it slide. I figured it was better to walk away than begin the first day by lunging at the throat of another guide. Deep breath. At that point all I wanted was to depart with a shred of professionalism and a clear idea of where I could take my sports without running into other boats. I just wanted to get on the river and go fishing.

My anglers today were two jovial guys in their early fifties with heavy Jersey accents. One guy tipped the scales (and my boat) at over 300 pounds, so balancing the weight took some extra time and forethought. Given my unexpected payload, I had to rethink my plan to wade some favorite shallow braids.

The wind was blowing sustained at 20 to 25 mph, but we got into some feisty rainbows early and stayed busy with them for the rest of the day. One guy was a decent caster, the other barely adequate; fortunately the fish are just plain easy this time of year.

The sun was shining, the river clear, and these two high school buddies spent the day laughing like kids and tossing private jokes back and forth across pools and seams hiding trout bigger than my arm.

They each hooked at least a dozen nice trout and landed a half dozen in the two-foot range. The big guy, who was struggling to get thirty feet in the gale, hooked a pig and fought it for about fifteen minutes before losing his balance, his tension on the line, and consequently the biggest trout of his life. It was the first time I've ever seen a colossal, Jersey Italian tough guy on the verge of tears.

The little guy, his buddy, after landing an especially gorgeous leopard-spotted buck, tenderly released the fish and turned to me with a grin that nearly split his face and his hypermasculine façade. "It's almost like a religious experience," he beamed.

Amen, brother.

JUNE 12

HERO GUIDING

The fishing has been spectacular for the past few days, which makes my job easy and enjoyable.

I live for opening week, a season full of promise and a fresh perspective not tainted by previous weeks and previous clients. By the end of the month we'll be into sockeye season, but the first week is pure. The trout are active, relatively untouched, aggressive, and huge. This is when we usually see our biggest rainbows of the season. Other watersheds in this region are known for their late-season trout, the big boys that follow the spawning salmon up past the lakes and gorge themselves into obesity on the rich and plentiful eggs. The sockeyes don't spawn in our part of the river, so we catch those same monster 'bows in June after they've finished spawning and are waiting for the big silver gravy train to lead them upriver.

So far none of my guys have stuck the thirty-inch trout. I've been waiting two seasons for it, but it hasn't happened yet. We usually get one or two a year, three if we're lucky, but we get lots of fish between twenty-five and twenty-eight inches. So far I've seen plenty of those, but the thirty-inch prize remains at large.

Finding fish during the first week is not especially challenging; if you can read water you can get into trout. Work the seams, the edges of gravel bars, the back sides of islands. If you fish the obvious lies with big undulating streamers, you'll have bent rods. It's fun, and the clients are happy, but after a few days of it I begin to get restless.

For me, the ultimate challenge is deciphering the fluid code of fish behavior that can mean the difference between a great day and an epic day. I want to find the fish that other people don't. I want to work the subtle gravel depressions that were overlooked by the guide who fished that beat the day before.

Does it really matter during opening week? No, not especially. My sports will have excellent fishing (probably the best of their lives) by simply working the obvious river structures. Still, though, while they're happily fishing the known spots, I'm trying to figure out the less obvious places where trout might hold. It will give me an advantage in a week or two after the easy holds have been heavily worked.

Right now, schools of salmon smolt are making their migration from the lakes down through the rivers to the ocean. They are plentiful, easy targets, and the rainbows take advantage of it. The young salmon are vulnerable during this trip and move downriver in massive groups. Safety in numbers. It's nature's way of ensuring that a percentage of the hatch survives the trip.

Lately I've been finding flocks of Arctic terns working the big gravel flats, and my Jersey goodfellas have had a blast casting Clouser minnows to pods of rainbows crashing baitfish like stripers. Just like offshore fishing, if you find the flocks of feeding birds, you find the bait. If you find the bait, you find the big fish eating the bait. They boil and thrash at the surface as they gobble up smolt in the shallow water. The sports love it because they can pick out targets as they move among the billowing clouds of immature salmon: make a cast . . . strip . . . strip . . . SET! And then the rod doubles over and two feet of trout comes cartwheeling across the river. It's fantastic, nearly as exciting as mouse fishing.

In this ecosystem there are a lot of mice and voles that live near the river; there are also large numbers of big, aggressive trout that will eat anything high in protein. When a rodent falls into the water and tries to kick his way back to the shore, there's a good chance that a big rainbow will catch up with him.

Right now the water is still cold, but when it warms into the mid-forties and low fifties, the trout will become more active and start chasing big flies tied with spun deer hair to imitate mice. Their low weight and high wind resistance make them difficult to cast but fun to fish. The floating vermin imitation skates across the water, leaving a gurgling wake that looks like an awkwardly swimming rodent. If the fisherman is lucky, a big mouth will open up behind the bulky fly and it will disappear with a sound like a toilet flushing.

We managed to catch one fish on a mouse pattern today, a small rainbow that must have been trying to get a jump on his larger relatives by eating big early. It hasn't yet reached the fever pitch that mouse fishing can become; I give it a week.

JUNE 14

THE DAY OF DAYS

There are two (silly, I admit) guiding goals that I set for myself this season. I'm not really a "numbers guy." In fact, I cringe at the term, just as many guides do. There's nothing worse than busting your ass for a person who catches nineteen fish in a day but considers that day a failure because he didn't catch twenty. I do, however, enjoy striving for an occasional quantifiable accomplishment that I can get really excited about.

As I mentioned earlier, I'd love to have a client catch a trout over thirty inches. It would also be cool to witness a double hookup that measures a combined four feet. Much of this is luck and if I never reach these arbitrary benchmarks I probably won't lose any sleep, but if one of them should occur, it would give me something extra to hoot and holler about on the river. It's a long season up here, and getting demonstratively excited is one of the things that keep me vibrant and upbeat throughout.

Today I ended up being an especially vibrant and upbeat guide because both of my goals were attained within the span of an hour.

It was one of those days when the river gods seemed to be choreographing everything around me in the best possible ways. I was paired with a couple of solid fishermen who were also a pleasure to spend nine hours with. This combination, in my line of work, is akin to a school bus driver having a morning commute without traffic or screaming children.

We drew the farthest beat from camp, a difficult stretch of river even at normal flows. During the high water we're currently experiencing, it's basically one long, flooded riffle. The river switches back and forth sharply, narrowing into a tight, lush canyon as you get farther upstream. The landscape shifts with the character of the water: it's heavily wooded, greener, and has more rise and fall than the flat, marshy scrub of the lower river. Most of the water is at least knee-deep and moving swiftly over large, slick boulders. It's a dramatic departure from the surefooted gravel bars that make up most of our water. It's an isolated beat, hard to fish unless you know it well, and it's the only piece of water we fish where you're guaranteed not to see another soul. If you go there with inexperienced clients, you can be in for a long day; if your anglers can cast, they might hook the fish of a lifetime.

The hour-long ride upriver in an uncovered johnboat can be cold and miserable. Today, though, was actually pleasant. We spotted a young sow brown bear and her three cubs, small fuzzy beings that reveal none of the volatile and destructive power they will soon develop. A little farther on we saw a gangly moose splashing across the river in front of us.

Wildlife viewing can break up an early-morning commute. It provides an excuse to slow the pace, to breathe deeply and focus on the beauty of the land. This happens only when the clients are open to a holistic fishing experience. Sometimes you get the sports that are too focused on the fish to even notice the lumbering majesty of a bear or the subtle beauty of spring tundra. From the outset, these guys immersed themselves in the total experience. They pointed out the bears with squeals and excitement more typical of six-year-olds than guys well over sixty. The fishing started slow, but neither of them seemed to care. They were enjoying the scenery and each other's company on a wild and spectacular section of river.

Around noon, the sun started to burn away the clouds and mist. As the water and our body temperatures began to warm, my anglers started hooking fish. A few were in the two-foot range but nothing spectacular for this area. I had them fishing about fifty yards apart. The upstream angler was fishing from shore, sight-casting to a nice rainbow holding in the shade beneath a patch of overhanging alders. My other client was working a deep bucket beneath a hard-pushing current. Together, we had eased our way over the greased boulders to get him into casting position, locking arms and moving slowly so that neither of us wound up swimming. I stayed with him because of the treacherous spot and he worked it hard. I knew it was holding fish, but he wasn't having any action. I put on a heavier streamer to get him down a bit deeper and stood on his left shoulder, coaching him into the right swing.

"Cast about fifteen feet to your right, give one big upstream mend, and let the fly swing back, through . . . THERE HE IS!"

He set the hook and the fish didn't move. After fifteen seconds it was still holding its ground at the bottom of the pool and I knew he was into something big—I wasn't sure how big but I had a good feeling. The heavy current forced frothing water up my thighs as I charged upstream to retrieve my net from the boat. When I got back several minutes later, he still hadn't seen the fish. It was lurking down in the bucket and doggedly resisting the pressure my client was applying. With calm determination, he stood with his back against the rushing water and continued to lean against the eight-weight fly rod in his hands. His partner had seen me go for the net and was now standing on the bank above us, witnessing the battle, rod at his side, smiling quietly.

When the fish finally gave up its lair in the bottom of the pool, it took several tries with my arms fully extended and my feet barely touching gravel to get it into the net. Goal number one had been reached: the massive rainbow taped out at thirty-one inches with a nineteen-inch girth. I guessed it to be about fifteen pounds—an ancient river buck still wearing his spawning scars and plumage. We took a few pictures and released it—well exercised but unharmed—into the pool that it was calling home. It was an incredible trout, the largest I've ever seen. I was downright giddy and I couldn't have imagined a client I'd rather see holding that fish.

Sadly, he has to leave tomorrow, two days before the rest of his crew. He's leaving early to pick up his wife from a cancer treatment center. His friends essentially kidnapped him for a week of fishing while his wife was away at treatment. "What was he gonna do, spend the whole time staring at the walls and tearing himself up?" they told me later.

He explained the situation, very matter-of-factly, after we shared the experience of his fish of a lifetime. He told me about the house they had just bought together, how she had picked out all the furniture and how he would have to change it if she died. He didn't look at me as he spoke; he just stared at the water and cast his line. I held the bow of the boat in my hands, arms straining as I worked it across the current. I watched my steps and remained quiet; he chose his words carefully. It was more like he was talking to the river than to me.

The mood was not soured by our conversation, but it made the day's success mean a little more. An hour after he caught the toad, he and his partner doubled up on twenty-five-inch rainbows. Around 3:00 p.m. the kidnapped man said the only thing he hadn't done yet was catch a fish on a mouse. We jetted back downriver for half an hour to my go-to mousing hole. It wasn't in our beat, so technically it was off limits. I can think of very few circumstances when I would have encroached on someone else's water, but this time I felt it was warranted. The river gods continued to smile on us: he landed three trout on the skating mouse fly in forty minutes. After releasing the third shiny rainbow into the cold water, he cut off the mouse, handed it back to me, and said he was ready for a cocktail and a cigar.

I don't usually smoke cigars, but I did partake in one tonight as we sat on the deck in the twilight and recounted the tale of the day's incredible fishing. The acrid tendrils of smoke swirled around us and kept the bugs at bay while our laughter echoed across the shivering river.

JUNE 15

CADDIS

The sun has shone for two days now, and the caddis have begun to wriggle from their watery casings. At mid-morning, with temperatures hovering in the seventies, I started seeing a few bugs on the water, so I had my guys reel in their sink tips and set out for a side channel that ends in a large, soft-water pool. There is no guaranteed dry-fly water on this river, but this stretch under these conditions is as close as it gets. I was pretty sure we would see the surface tension broken with the splashy attacks of grayling—and I was hoping for at least one rainbow, but I wasn't expecting a healthy interspersing of subtly sipping trout.

I parked the boat on the edge of the main current, and we bushwhacked through some marshy thickets to approach a still-water pool that sits off the main stem of the river. I tried to keep the clients from getting too excited or anxious, telling them that we would probably see only grayling but to keep their eyes open for anything larger. We approached with more stealth than is actually necessary (the fish here are generally unwary), but subtle theatrics can add to the overall experience and enhance the feeling of success that results from landing a large trout on a dry fly. We crouched in the high grass and waited for a thick green back to show itself. Specifically, we watched the far side of the pool where the currents swirl and make for a nearly impossible drift.

Within the first minute, a big snout poked through the film not ten feet from where we were hunkered. I had an excellent angler with me, and he began gingerly flipping casts in the area of the rise form. Five casts later he was hooked into a beautiful two-foot buck that tail-danced its way around the pool and pulled his underpowered four-weight into a half circle.

The dry-fly fishing on this river is like teenage sex: uncertain and short-lived, but damn exciting when you get some. We'll be lucky to get trout on dries six days out of the season; today was the first. The grayling are more predictable. We can count on them to be dimpling and popping for another month or so, eating lime sallies and other stray bugs. The caddis hatch is by far the most prolific and the only one with enough protein to distract the trout from gorging on salmon fry and baby lampreys.

I'll enjoy it while it lasts and try not to be too disheartened when it evaporates.

JUNE 16

AND ON THE NINTH DAY I SHOWERED

Yeah, it was about time. I've been called a smelly bastard before (lots of times, actually), but when someone you consider to be an odoriferous dirtbag calls you a smelly bastard, that's saying something.

My buddy Dillis did just that today—I admit, I saw it coming. You know it's bad when you can smell yourself; you know it's worse when you can't stand the smell of yourself unless fully clothed. I was just about there. I'm not opposed to showering; in fact, I enjoy a nice hot shower. But the convenience factor is simply lacking here: I can't just walk down the hall and hop in the shower. I have to make an event out of it and I just don't have much time or energy for any more events in my day. Yeah, I have a couple of hours in the evening, but there are other, more important things to do: tie flies, drink a couple beers with my buddies, and tap on this silly keyboard. Showering just slips on the priority list. When I do make time for it, there's usually someone else in there or we're out of hot water.

When the water heater tank is empty, "cold" doesn't begin to describe the liquid that flows from our stained shower-head. It's pumped directly from a spring-fed well buried beneath the frost layer of the tundra. Adjectives like *icy, polar, glacial,* and *bone-chilling* come to mind.

Cold showers are only a minor inconvenience when one is generally warm. Say, for example, it's summertime in the south or it's the dead of winter in the Dakotas and you're blessed with balmy indoor heating. But when you guide all day out in the cold and you sleep all night in a cold tent, a frigid shower is the kind of experience that might erode the last vestige of an already tenuous state of sanity.

Basically, it makes me want to take my next bath in the river, in front of the camp, just in time for the after-dinner cigar crowd (who used up all the hot water) so they can see firsthand the effects of cold-water bathing on the body.

Okay, these are all just excuses. Maybe I like the fact that I shower only once a week when I'm up here. Perhaps I get some weird ego charge by bathing less frequently than men who consider personal hygiene something to be attended to as a necessity. Maybe I just like the fact that being in the middle of nowhere without any women gives me an excuse not to shower. Maybe I'm just an odoriferous dirtbag, like Dillis.

More likely, it's the lack of women.

JUNE 17

EGO TRIPPIN'

Fishing guides, especially those who guide in Alaska, tend to have egos even bigger than their hat collections. We all consider ourselves pretty much hot shit. I mean, it's kind of necessary if you think about it. You have to think somewhat highly of yourself to charge other people lots of money just for the privilege of fishing with you. We try not to perch on the gate and crow in front of the clients (most of us, anyway); but behind closed doors the professional veneer falls away and we puff and strut like fighting cocks in a trailer park.

As in any other social network, there's an established pecking order within our staff, and we mostly stay within our implied boundaries. The head guide can say whatever the fuck he wants and the new guys better keep their heads down, their mouths shut, and their feet moving. In between, there's some gray area, and that's where you get the elbowing and shoving.

These dynamics are made all the more interesting by the remote nature of our existence. We are not shop guides in the Lower 48 who take their clients out for the day, drop them off, and go home. We are all dependent upon one another. You may get into a shouting match with a guy one night because he pinched off your water or took a net from your boat without asking, and then the next morning you're trusting him with your life. It's a strange community of ego and testosterone tempered by the necessity of symbiosis.

Most of us are extremely good at what we do, but I have no illusions about what that actually entails. We're not brain surgeons; we're fishing guides, but we're fishing guides in a wild and remote part of the world. We spin flies, suggest casts and mends, tie knots, and net fish. If that knot fails or a loop collapses or a hook is thrown; if that fish slips out of the net, it's not the end of the world, no one will die. But if a boat nails a rock at high speed or a hook dives into an eye; if a man in his eighties loses his footing and slips into the river, it might feel like the end of the world and someone might die.

I guess we're cocky because our clients are gambling a great deal on the belief (or the hope) that we'll provide the fishing trip of a lifetime—and most of us routinely rise to that challenge. I can take you up the river, put you where the fish are, help you make the right cast, net the fish of your dreams, bring you home safely, and take pictures of the whole experience. But if I'm not absolutely sure of that when I get out of bed each morning, it's going to be a long day.

JUNE 19

THE COMEDOWN

The majesty of the first week couldn't continue. I knew that, on some level, all along. We had good weather, great clients, and epic fishing. Such a trifecta is rarely achieved and has set me up for disappointment from here on out.

The weather has held, even improved. It's been in the seventies and sunny for two days in a row, a feat not achieved all of last season. As for the other factors that ultimately define our success . . . well, at least the weather has held.

I have guided a couple in their mid-seventies for the past two days. She is extremely sweet, almost saccharine. She's like a Midwestern grandmother who gardens, and bakes, and cares for children and animals—and never, ever stops talking about those activities. He's a little gruffer but a truly nice man. As companions to spend a day with they are really wonderful, but they can't wade past their ankles and they can't cast more than fifteen feet. This makes catching fish a bit challenging. I've spent most of the past two days walking the boat along gravel bars and swinging it back and forth in the high-water current while they hold their rods. Yes, I am a human trolling motor. You do what you have to do to catch fish. I'm sore as hell, but their rods are often bent and when they aren't bickering at one another they seem to be having a good time.

"Shelley, get your rod tip up."

"I'm doing what the guide told me to do, Ron—now leave me alone."

"But your rod tip isn't high enough; you're going to lose him."

"Ron, this is why we have a guide. I'm listening to what he tells me to do. Now you just worry about your fish."

"Oh, you see there? You see what I told you? Now you lost him 'cause you had your rod down."

"I lost him because you won't stop pestering me. If you're going to do this every day, I'm not going to fish with you anymore. You can just go by yourself and I'll get the guide to take me out alone."

It has gone on like this for two days now. It's amusing but exhausting, and my view of marriage is becoming tainted.

Guided fishing trips are NOT about the guide. My experience is secondary, though some days I'll admit that I forget this. My primary focus is for people to enjoy their day on the river, and this won't happen unless I'm enjoying the day as well. My job is to remain upbeat regardless of how many fish are caught—or not caught due to missed strikes, blown casts, inept wading, etc. I'm usually able to smile and hoot regardless of the day or the client, but I do have to bite my tongue when asked a question like the one Ron asked today while I struggled to hold the boat in the current with one hand and net a fish for him with the other.

"So, Miles, when am I going to catch that twenty-seven-incher that I came all the way up here for?"

"Oh, he's out there. We just have to keep working at it."

JUNE 20

NOT MY FINEST HOUR

Simply put, it was a tough day and my dog was there to see it. My clients today requested that we bring Lehua with us in the boat. She rode on the front casting platform most of the day, her legs spread in a wide stance and her ears flapping in the breeze.

The water has warmed and the rainbows have begun aggressively chasing mice. One of my clients got into about twenty fish on mouse patterns today. Oh, and the other client? She caught one trout . . . one trout all day. She hooked a great deal more than that, but the fact remains: she landed one trout in nine hours. This is not acceptable from my perspective. One client had a consistently bent rod and the other had to watch fish after fish slide into the net while holding a perpetually flaccid line.

I put her in the honey holes; I coached her all day. It just wasn't happening. By 1:00 p.m. she and I both needed to take a cookie break and scratch the dog's ears. The variant success rates mirrored the skill levels of the two clients, but I'm supposed to act as an equalizer of sorts. Today I failed.

Beyond my personal malfunction, every goddamn fly-out lodge within a hundred miles has heard about our fishing, and our normally placid river is teeming with migrant mouth-breathers. They're watching where we fish and then mimicking our movements the next day. One guy low-holed me three times today—three times! Normally I would have let that go, but I was already frustrated. I finally got out of my boat, left my clients fishing, walked downriver to him, and asked if I could have a word with him. We walked out of earshot of his sports before I gave him an unsolicited lesson that began, "I don't know what the etiquette is on your river, but on this river . . ."

Turns out the guy owns a very successful lodge near here and has been guiding these waters since I was in grade school. It was a pointless thing to do and I acted like an asshole, but it made me feel better. He wants the same thing I want: to help people catch fish. That's his job, too. Our interaction won't change the dynamic on the river. If anything, it will make him intentionally low-hole me whenever he can. I immediately regretted the decision, more so when I later found out who he was. The whole experience, along with the imbalance of fish-catching between my clients, kind of threw my chi out of whack.

Such a day of fishing would stand alone as rather unpleasant, but it progressed from bad to terrible on the way back to camp when my motor died less than a mile from the dock.

Why?

Because I forgot to put oil in it yesterday.

The only two things that you absolutely, positively cannot forget to put in your engine are gas and oil. It doesn't get much more basic than that. I was flushed with embarrassment when I had to flag down Dillis as he passed us on his way home. He took my clients back for me and returned with some oil.

I wonder if there's a surgery to remove one's head from one's ass? Probably not this far out in the bush.

JUNE 22

SOGGY SOLITUDE

Sitting in the outhouse in a wet raincoat is a miserable experience. The water runs off the PVC and onto various areas that I prefer warm and dry. The monsoons have come; I knew they would. The oasis of warm, sunny weather simply could not continue.

Forty-eight hours of rain has washed away all remnants of my early-season elation. We're back into my favorite cycle: guide for nine hours in the rain, come back to camp, build in the rain until eleven, pass out, wake up, and repeat. This evening I slunk off to the shitter three times because I just wasn't feeling motivated to participate in soggy, unending labor.

Because I was feeling a little low (and the weather sucks), I pulled my stash of fingerless fleece gloves out of my fishing bag this morning. For half an hour they were dry and glorious. I removed them and carefully hid them in my pockets to net and release fish, hoping to extend the experience of warmth on my hands. Eventually the misting rain overwhelmed them, and my hands were soaked and cold for the rest of the day. Dry gloves for fishing guides around here are like blowjobs for married guys: you don't get to experience them very often, so when you do, you have to enjoy them thoroughly. I basked in the momentary bliss that they provided before untying another "wind knot" and repeating, for the eighteenth time that morning, "Tighten up your line before you start your back cast and that won't happen."

JUNE 25

THE FLOOD

The downpours finally stopped last night, but the water has risen nearly a foot in the past two days. This change has seriously hampered the fishing. Many of our most productive gravel bars are now submerged, and the area of fishable water has greatly diminished.

On the brighter side, the flood has chased off all the fly-out guys, so we now have a bit more room to spread out—like thirty miles. The river gods have also left us with a few hatching bugs, and the twenty-three-incher that took a caddis on the last cast left a sugar coating on an otherwise bland day. It was the only rise that we saw, but it was the only one we needed.

The problem with guiding is that it gives me too much time to think. I spend the majority of my day standing in or beside the river, watching other people fish. When I'm actually fishing, my mind is occupied while I soak in the outdoors and fall into the repetitive hypnosis of the activity. When guiding, I don't have the physical, rhythmic routine of casting, mending, drifting, or stripping to pacify my overactive mind.

Seventy percent of the time I'm focusing on the job at hand: what people are doing with their casts and how they're working the water. Are they wading too deep? Are there any fish rising? Is there a bear about to eat one of my sports?

The remaining time I'm lost in my own thoughts. I'm thinking about the girlfriend I broke up with before I left; I'm remembering the tear-streaked anger in her face. I'm tallying how much money I owe the IRS. Should I get a graduate degree? Does it suck that I'm pushing thirty and have no equity? How cool do those clouds look when they push down off the mountains into our valley? Why do I always run away from anything long-term—like when I graduated from college, broke up with my girlfriend, quit my job, and moved to Africa? Where would I be now if I had stayed?

Probably not in this chilly-damp place where it's still light outside at midnight.

Thirty percent of a nine-hour day is a long time to stew in one's own cerebral juices. I guess it's better than sitting behind a desk, though. If I had stayed in that job and kept that life, I'd probably be spending eighty-five percent of my time daydreaming about doing something like this.

JUNE 26

ETHICS

From time to time I find myself spiraling into ethical dilemmas over what I do for a living. Don't get me wrong: I love what I do. I love the river and its constant rebirth, but sometimes my ability to justify my work is eclipsed by thoughts of the historical precedent of humans exploiting wild and fragile ecosystems.

If I look at this honestly, I'm doing nothing more than peddling myself and one of our country's greatest fisheries. We are whoring out the river and its fish to glean a profit. I don't have a problem with that concept as a whole. Many fisheries elsewhere in the country would not exist if not for the strong support (vocally and monetarily) of the outfitters and guides who dredge their livings from those waterways. The funds generated by license fees and the conservation projects supported by avid fishermen are what keep many rivers alive. That's not the case here; we're not stewards of a watershed threatened by agriculture or development.

This is an extractive enterprise—not too unlike mining or drilling for oil, which are industries I routinely decry. Though this comparison may be extreme, it is still valid. I'm not saying that sportfishing has had nearly the environmental impact of either of those industries, but we're still taking a natural resource (fish) and exploiting it for profit.

This watershed was once populated by sparse native settlements; now it's mostly federally protected with a few private native allotments. The owner of our camp purchased one of these native allotments and now owns a piece of land surrounded by government property.

We bring in anglers from around the country and drive them around this wilderness area in jet boats, burning petroleum products and spewing exhaust. We try to minimize our impact by running four-stroke engines, and we have an elaborate system to keep as much gas and oil out of the river as possible. We do everything within our control to keep the water clean, but there is also concern for the riverbanks and gravel bars.

A study was done by the park service a few years back to determine the effects of boat wakes on the river course. Granted, while no single set of small waves carrying grains of pulverized rock downstream matters greatly, the sum total of an entire fleet or season certainly might. While the researchers did find that powerboats were contributing to erosion, they also found that bears tramping along the banks and looking for salmon had a far greater effect. There's a delicate balance up here; I'm sure that if the park service had to make a choice, it would kick us out and let the bears stay.

With respect to the fish, we require that our sports use single barbless hooks, and we have a zero-harvest limit on trout. Sadly, some of those incredible trout die despite our best efforts to release them alive. Anyone who's seen a client fumble a six-pound rainbow headfirst onto the floor of an aluminum johnboat and then chuck it over the side knows exactly what I'm talking about. But people want pictures of their trophies—and with the money they've spent, how can I blame them? Who am I to judge? I take their tip money and grin and shake their hands—and then behind their backs I moan about their lack of respect for the resource. After I wave good-bye to them, I repeat the drill with the next group of anglers that flies in to take a bite out of the Alaskan wilderness.

I know that I wouldn't even be here if not for the people that pay to come fishing; I probably wouldn't even know this place existed. I don't try to pretend that fishing is friendly to the fish—technically it's a blood sport. I'm well aware of this and I'm okay with it. But I just don't really see how any of us who come here to guide or fish are truly entitled to exploit this incredibly unique ecosystem. Occasionally I stub my toe on that nagging issue.

I'm certainly more aware of problems than solutions. I see a multitude of ominous, impending fates hanging over the coastal fisheries of southwestern Alaska. For now, they loom above, having not yet changed from dark, abstract ruminations into sharp, hopeless realities. The rivers are still running clean and the salmon are maintaining the fragile balance of the ecosystem. I only hope that I'm not contributing too much to their ultimate demise.

THE SALMON ARE LATE

They should have been here by now, but they're not—and the reports we're getting from downriver indicate that they won't be here anytime soon.

I've seen two random migrants so far, dark torpedoes that wriggled past me so quickly they could have been mistaken for a trick of light and shadow. But the late sockeye run isn't completely bad because we're still catching rainbows, and I'm happy for that. It's only a matter of time, though, before the sockeye surge scatters the trout and makes them tough to find. In some stretches of river they're already thinning out, and a few guides have had some slow trout days.

Granted, it's all relative, and a tough day here could be a good day elsewhere, but you have to consider the expectations of the people we take fishing. They've paid big dollars and traveled great distances. Their expectations are high, and if I can't produce some big fish, or at least a fair number of good-size fish, the day throbs with an undercurrent of disappointment.

To avoid such awkwardness, I've been cogitating some new strategies to get people into trout until the salmon arrive and we switch from being guides to fish processors. The way I see it, the trout are still in the river (obviously), but their food sources and their preferred holding waters are changing. The clouds of salmon smolt and baby lampreys have moved on through, and the bug hatches are tapering off. Streamers and dry flies are no longer as effective, so I'm planning to work on some nymphing techniques until the salmon move in. Nymphs are flies that imitate the under-water life phase of aquatic insects. They are the main tactic for catching trout in most rivers, but nearly unheard of in this camp.

Tomorrow I plan to break out my subsurface bug boxes, slide some bobbers on leaders, pinch on some split shot, and set some guys up in the riffles for a little high-sticking. Every guide in the Lower 48 is using the same technique to catch the smaller cousins of the brutes we're targeting, so why not here?

I'm just happy to continue chasing trout for a few more days before the mindless slaughter begins.

JUNE 30

A SUCCESSFUL EXPERIMENT

I left the dock this morning with an optimistic outlook and my nymphing gear in tow. I didn't tell my clients what I had in mind. I let them pound the first run with streamers while I sat in the boat and strung up a bobber rod. They picked up three relatively small trout on the big meaty flies we've been using all season.

I stepped from the boat and handed the rod I had just rigged up to the closest guy, telling him I wanted to try something a little different. He's an experienced trout fisherman and is familiar with nymphing; he was happy to play guinea pig. In half an hour he caught three trout over twenty inches from the same water that had just been fished with a streamer rig.

We had a fantastic day, and it was a nice way for the clients to finish off their week of fishing—lots of action and some very respectable fish to the net. For me it was just nice to have a theory actually work out. So often in fly fishing I have these conjectures, moments of epiphany in which I'm certain I've cracked the secret of a particular stream, or hatch, or fish species—only to be thwarted by reality.

At the end of the day, I cut off everybody's leaders and swore my guys to secrecy about our method of fishing. I'll tell a few other guides, but there's a particular guide on our staff whom

I'd like to see floundering around while others are catching consistently. He's a pompous narcissist who arrived the day before the clients because manual labor was not in his contract. He scoffed at the mention of nymphing and told me that big trout wouldn't eat subsurface insects on this river.

JULY 3

SLAUGHTERHOUSE FIVE

Fishing for sockeye salmon, in my opinion, is the lowest form of fly fishing that exists. Yes, you're using a fly rod and an artificial fly—but in many ways, drowning worms with a Zebco and a big orange bobber is more sporting. At least those fish are actively seeking your presentation.

One can call what we're doing "lining," or "flossing"—which has a healthy, positive connotation that I find amusing—but I prefer to call it what it really is: snagging fish in the face. I have, on occasion, seen sockeyes turn and intentionally eat a fly, but those occurrences are extremely rare. Those who are good at the "technique" will hook ninety percent of their fish in the corner of the jaw. And sadly I must include myself in this group as a result of professional necessity. But the fact remains: YOU ARE SNAGGING THEM IN THE FACE!

For those who may not be familiar with the process, let me explain it. One needs a stout rod (a ten- or eleven-weight is best) and a ten-foot leader with enough lead split shot to match the water depth and speed of the current. Sockeye flies are usually heavy-gauge offset hooks sparsely wrapped in yarn, Estaz, chenille, or pocket lint. Strip out about four feet of fly line, chunk it in the river, and swing the setup through a line of sockeyes swimming upstream with their mouths open. They always have their mouths open, so your odds of hooking up are pretty good.

The sockeyes push through our section of river on their way to the spawning beds up near the lake. Unlike the other species of salmon, they don't spend much time resting in the slow-water pools; they need a lake to sustain their young, so they don't stop until they hit still water. Because you're fishing to a constantly moving parade of salmon, you can't spook them or turn them off like you can the other species. They just keep coming.

For the next three to four weeks the sockeye run will continue past our lodge. During the peak flow, they'll be lined up tip to tail—an organic, fluttering procession extending six to ten feet from the north bank out toward the center of the river. They hold to the bank to stay out of the main current and conserve energy. For some reason (I can't get an answer on why this is true) they prefer the north bank.

Each day we assemble a small army of sports on a north-side gravel bar and let the lead fly. Each man can keep five fish a day. We'll sometimes put ten clients in line with three guides, which means we can take fifty fish. The guides don't get to take limits. For the entire day, at least three of those fishermen will be hooked up at any given time. All will be fighting a five- to twelve-pound salmon, fresh from the ocean, extremely strong, and pissed off.

Tenuously contained chaos is good description of the event. Lines cross with fishermen splashing around one another trying to keep their prize from wrapping up in someone else's rig. We show people how to properly hook the fish in the mouth, but many get snagged elsewhere. When a hook tears free from a lunging sockeye's dorsal or tail, a whipping bolo of lead, line, and sharp metal comes flying back toward the gravel bar. I've been known to hit the deck. In between all the ducking and scrambling, numerous fish are being landed and assessed. If too small, they're released; if not, they're swiftly bonked on the head, slashed at the gills, and put on a stringer to be filleted. Two of the three guides will be in the thick of the fray, netting fish, retying leaders, and removing hooks from flesh (human and salmon). Meanwhile the third guide is running a very sharp knife along the backbones of recently killed fish, washing the bright orange flesh in the river, bagging it, and assembling fillets in coolers.

I'll admit that it can be fun for a few days, but it gets old quickly. What blows my mind is the number of relatively good fly fishermen who love doing this. It lacks all of the challenge that fishing with a fly rod embodies. You don't even have to cast! I also don't understand how an intelligent person doesn't realize that he's force-feeding these fish. These are guys who have caught fish all over the world; yet after six days of this mindless chaos they'll still naively ask, "So what color do you think will work best today?"

"Oh, green is always good on cloudy days."

I just happened to have a great deal of green yarn at my tying bench, so that's the color I used the night before.

Today was the first day of sockeye fishing, and luckily I had to do it for only a half day. I got to spend the afternoon chasing trout because both of my sports decided this was not an activity they wanted to pursue for an extended period. I do know, however, that I'll be spending a great deal of this month with a bonking stick and a fillet knife tucked in my wading belt and a big, nylon mesh net in my bloody, fishy hands.

If there's any consolation to the brain-numbing madness of sockeye fishing, it's the opportunity to break rank from the lunchtime drudgery of turkey sandwiches and processed snacks.

Today's lunch was a welcomed change. Those sweet and firm fillets, fresh from the river, were delicious with a bit of lemon pepper, some seasoned salt, and caramelized onion.

We only had to chase off one family of bears to eat them in peace.

JULY 4

INDEPENDENCE DAY, INDEED

Freedom! Freedom from the oppression and carnage of sockeye fishing; that's what I celebrated today. That and four rainbows over twenty-four inches to the net, two of which measured over twenty-seven. I even got to relax a bit today because I was training our newest and most talkative guide, Dan. Luckily Dan had clients to jabber with, so I was mostly spared today's verbal avalanche.

Dan did most of the work, and I just rode along and told him when he was about to make a mistake. For example: "Hey Dan, watch out for that huge rock you're about to drive the boat over." He then frantically spun the tiller, barely missed he rock, and mumbled some excuse about the boat pulling to the right.

Things rolled along smoothly until the very end of the day, mostly because I was there to inform Dan when he was about to do something monumentally stupid. The clients were very laid back, and I even got to catch a couple of trout myself at their encouragement. This can be a sticky situation. Many people will tell you they want you to fish, but in reality they don't. They want you to appear to be fishing, but they also want you to be there at their beck and call, which means you're not really fishing. You're actually just standing near them and casting (preferably in water they've already fished) while waiting for them to need your assistance. And if you do happen to hook a big fish, you had better break it off; your client might pretend to be excited, but he'll be hiding some animosity.

At the very last hole, Dan had taken a client around the bend to fish one gravel bar while I stayed with the other sport and fished a deep trough. Dan was about ten minutes late bringing the boat to pick us up; when he finally pulled around the point, I could see immediately that something was up.

His first words to me were, "You're going to be so pissed at me."

So I figured it wasn't good.

"We lost your net, but we got a pig and we got pictures of it."

My brand-new—barely a week old—Brodin boat net was the net to which he referred. The net for which I had waited four weeks. The net that cost me far more than I'm willing to publicly admit. I winced internally; I couldn't visibly display my displeasure. I swallowed it because it would have spoiled the atmosphere surrounding the best day of fishing these clients may ever have. We searched fruitlessly around the gravel bars downstream but it was gone, consumed by the river.

I'll order a new one and he'll pay for it—but, seriously, you can't just drop a net in the current to take a picture of a fish, even if it's a pig. That's one expensive rookie mistake for him, and it means I'm stuck using the worthless plastic measure nets for another month . . . dammit.

JULY 10

LIVING THE DREAM

Ever since I learned that there was such a thing as a fishing guide, I knew that I wanted to be one. I even tried to present a convincing argument to my father detailing the wastefulness of spending so much time in a classroom. I think I was about ten. We were in the car on our way to school and Pink Floyd's *Another Brick in the Wall, Part II* came on the radio. I used that as fodder for reinforcing my position against formal education. He refuted me by pointing out that I didn't attend a draconian British boarding school. That led to another eleven years of textbooks and lectures.

I am living a childhood dream. I try to remind myself of this at least once daily. Like many of you reading this, I love being outside, on a river, surrounded by wilderness, with fish lurking in their haunts below the surface. Fishing is my faith-based activity and this is my sanctuary: a quiet place for a loud mind. Since I'm using the religious comparison already, I might as well affirm that rivers are my church; they're my places of peace and safe haven. That being the case, wilderness Alaska is my Jerusalem, my Vatican—a place that is the archetype of something sacred but somewhat flawed by the conflicting desires and beliefs of those who love it.

I wish I could say that I am perpetually serene living beside this river for four months out of the year, but much of the time I'm distracted with the details. I'm frustrated with the flushed and rotund orb of bedlam that runs this place. I'm frustrated with the erratic schedules and breezy changes of strategy that create twice the work for an already overworked staff. I worry about late paychecks, or finding employment when I return, or how to create and maintain a stable existence when I choose to walk out on it for one third of the year. I find myself reading and rereading *The Unbearable Lightness of Being.*

I recognize the dream attained, and I try each day to hold that candle cupped against the wind of flaky employers, bitter e-mails from angry ex-girlfriends, expectations of success (financial and otherwise), monofilament cuts in the crevices of my fingers, and groups of meat-hungry fishermen giving me dirty looks when they snap twenty-five-pound leaders at my blood knot.

I'm not yet ready to wake up, but dreams lose some of their magic once you realize that you're dreaming and you try to milk more out of it before the alarm goes off.

JULY 12

THE FRENCH CANADIAN CONNECTION

Our camp this week has been invaded by six different French-speaking families that have come to Alaska in search of adventure, coolers filled with salmon, and stories to tell their friends and neighbors when they get home. They will not be disappointed.

Our standard clientele are post-middle-aged men on vacation with other men. Fish camps, like hunting camps, are not traditionally viewed as places for the mixing of genders. Many of the men who spend their vacations here are enjoying a reprieve from the stresses of their lives. As sad a statement as it may be about the matrimonial status of these guys, that also includes a break from the women and families they purport to love. Unfortunately, our majority male clientele means that we who work here for seventeen weeks each summer are deprived of the opportunity to interact with the fairer sex.

The Canadian group arrived as a mixed bag of husbands, wives, sons, and (yes, it's true) daughters. When clients arrive downriver, a guide is always right beside the plane offering a hand in case someone is unsteady walking on the narrow floats. We also offer stability and assistance boarding the boats and stepping off onto the dock. One of us always attends to this, but this is the first week that I've seen guides rushing in front of each other to offer their gallantry.

To be perfectly frank, a couple of the wives are downright hot. There's no point in denying it; they have been the talk of the camp since the day they arrived. One of these voluptuous beauties brought along her blossoming spawn: a dark-haired young woman with extremely tight shirts and a glimmering nose stud who immediately drew attention from the younger set of male employees. The first night at dinner she sat next to Dillis and shamelessly flirted with him throughout the meal. Giggling at his wit, she let her hand flutter to rest on his shoulder, and I could see the familiar pattern of charm that I've seen play out in many bars.

The next day she and her family were assigned to his boat, and Dillis strutted to the dock bright and early with a particularly springy step. That evening he was reticent; I found him sitting alone in his Weatherport staring at the ceiling. I handed him one of the two lukewarm cans of beer I was carrying. Refrigerator space is limited, so we drink our beer at room (tent) temperature. We sat for a moment in awkward silence. I finally spoke up when it became obvious that he wasn't planning to volunteer any information.

"You're one lucky bastard."

"What do you mean?"

"You know what I mean. You had the hotties in your boat, and Dick told me they loved you so much they've requested you for the rest of the week."

He maintained the silence, staring at the wall and sipping his beer. I pressed on.

"Even in waders I bet those women look damn good."

"Yep."

"So how old is she?"

"Hmmm?"

"The daughter, bro—the one you were flirting with. Don't play dumb with me."

"I wasn't flirting."

"Bullshit."

"I wasn't."

"She can't be more than twenty-two. She's way too young for you."

"Actually, she's fifteen."

I nearly sprayed Budweiser out my nostrils and onto his pile of rank laundry. I couldn't believe it. The girl not only had a body curved with maturity but she carried herself with a confidence and femininity that I certainly don't remember from the girls in my high school.

"Fifteen! Dude!"

"I'm not gonna do anything."

"Damn right you're not. That would be wrong on so many levels—and you'd be breaking Ken's number one rule."

He turned toward me and cracked a smile. When I caught his eye, we both erupted in laughter. There aren't too many things you can do to get fired from a remote lodge that needs a full staff to run smoothly, but screwing a client is one of them. Every year at the beginning of the season Ken gives us his sex speech, and it always ends the same way: "It's only four months; just keep your damn dick in your pants."

Dillis spent the rest of the week batting around the flirtatious volleys of a well-endowed teenager. There were bets in camp on how long it would be before he cracked and broke Ken's rule. Despite the fact that an old friend once described Dillis as "the horniest man alive," my money was on him taking it no farther than a healthy helping of harmless banter.

As far as I know, that was the extent of it— though I'm relatively certain that Dillis would have jumped all over an opportunity to play slap and tickle with the girl's mother.

FRIDAY THE THIRTEENTH

Despite the superstitious tradition that suggests otherwise, today turned out to be a lucky day for me. Today I got a small respite from the grind, just enough to recharge the batteries ever so slightly. Enough to keep me the positive, enthusiastic person that my job and my sanity necessitate.

Because of the nature of this place and this job, I have been working ten to fifteen hours every day for the past fifty some-odd days, straight. Since June 8 I've guided thirty-one days. I'm not complaining; I knew the deal when I signed on, but still a person gets to be a little burned. The smile muscles, not to mention the rest of the body, get a little tired.

Today our camp full of French Canadians took a day off from slaughtering salmon and flew to Brooks Falls for some Disneyland-type bear viewing. We expected that there would be some project created for us: building something, fixing something, digging something—and indeed that was the plan. However, last night at the staff meeting Paul spoke up on behalf of all of us and negotiated a worthy compromise. We got a half day off. So we had until noon to do whatever we wanted, after which we had to paint, fill fish boxes, etc. I slept until 8:30 a.m.—eight-thirty! This experience was so pleasant that it was almost guilty, like adolescent masturbation.

I could have slept much later, but I only had until noon. And while I spend nearly every day on the river with other people who are fishing, I never get to go fishing. For me, going fishing means spending water-soluble moments and hours that diffuse into casts, mends, drifts, and long stares with my thoughts whittling away at nothing more meaningful than where I think a fish or two might be hiding. There's a difference between trying to find fish for yourself and finding them for someone who's paying a great deal of money to have you find fish.

For a couple of hours, until the noon work whistle sounded, I went trout fishing with my friend Paul. We were unhurried. We talked a little, we fished a lot, and we belly-laughed. This morning I looked upon the landscape that I work in with a greater ability to imbibe its beauty.

I can't say that we had a great day of catching, but the fishing was spectacular. The trout are a bit tough to find with all the sockeyes pushing them around, but we each caught our share.

At our last stop of the morning, we parked the boat on an island with a long gravel bar extending downstream. Between the island and the shore was a waist-deep channel about forty feet wide. I had crossed and was standing on the south bank working into the current. Paul was on the gravel bar fishing back toward the bank. He broke my spell of casting when he yelled across the rushing water, "Hey, look at the moose!"

I looked upstream and saw a brown shape in the water, but I could tell it was no moose. It was a bear swimming across the main channel of the river toward the island.

"That's a bear!"

Just after the words left my mouth, a young bull moose crashed through the trees on the island, exploded into the channel above me, and went bounding off across the tundra. I realized what was happening when I looked back to see the bear, intent on its quarry, swimming a course that would land it on the gravel bar directly between Paul and the boat.

I yelled at him. "It's coming right at you!"

"Not anymore. It just took off across the tundra." Paul hadn't even noticed the pursuing bear; he was too focused on the departing moose.

"No, the bear!" I yelled back at him, pointing wildly upstream. He spun around and finally saw the approaching predator, but the bear hadn't even noticed us. It was chugging across the swift flow of the river, hoping to catch up to that tasty, young moose.

The distance between the grizzly and Paul and the boat was closing quickly. I was stranded on the far side of the channel and incapable of doing anything but yelling. Paul paused, momentarily, and weighed his options. Wisely, he began splashing upstream toward both the bear and the johnboat, yelling and waving his arms. Startled by Paul's aggressive advance, the bear spun around in the current and fled toward the bank from which it had come.

Apparently these bears have a short attention span and no capacity at all for frustration by failure (I could take a lesson). Before it even reached the far side of the river, it plunged its head beneath the surface and began snorkeling for salmon.

The bear didn't get its moose, but Paul and I got our daily shot of adrenaline and a good story to tell everyone at dinner.

JULY 14

FOOD FIGHT

The chef gave his two weeks' notice today. The chef, you know—
the guy who makes all our food. His dramatic departure has been a
brewing possibility for some time now. He, Ken, and Francine have
been circling each other with thinly stretched smiles and a flimsy
veneer of respect for at least a week. Their clash of personalities
was like an open ocean wind swell raging across a breaker reef.

Our early-morning meal is normally a somber and groggy
event. People may grumble quietly about the breakfast menu, their
sports, or their assigned beat for that day, but on most mornings
we're generally a benign and understated group. Today, though, our
breakfast was a bit more exciting.

Ken sat down in the yurt to eat breakfast with the staff
this morning and was horrified to discover that the waffles included
breakfast sausage and whole wheat. "What the hell is this crap?" he
growled. "Where does this guy think he is? Our clients don't want
to eat this shit. They want their fucking waffles and their fucking
sausage on different parts of the goddamn plate!"

He got louder and redder with every sentence. The line
of flush crept up his face and onto his scalp and when it disappeared beneath his hairline, he exploded.

"I'm sick of this shit! This is my goddamn camp and

I'm gonna tell him straight up what he can and cannot cook. If he thinks this is what our clients want—"

His words were drowned out by the sound of slamming doors and stomping feet as he made his way out of the yurt and into the kitchen. We continued to eat in silence, listening to the muted exchange vibrating through the walls. I couldn't decipher any words, but the tone wasn't friendly. After a minute or two Ken slammed and stomped his way back to the yurt. Puffed up and self-satisfied, he sat back down at the table. "Maybe now we'll get a normal goddamn breakfast."

Some grumbles of approval rose from the bleary-eyed crowd.

"'Bout time."

"Hope so."

Dick spoke up without raising his eyes from his picked apart, half-eaten yuppie waffle. "Hey, Ken, could you get him to cook the sausage a little longer?"

JULY 15

CHARACTERS

We have a unique group in camp this week. The ring-leader and financier (we'll call him Jake) has been fishing up here with Ken for fifteen years, since this place was only four tents and two guides.

Jake is a very wealthy individual who runs a successful factory business. Every year he brings a group of twenty or so with him—mainly his blue-collar employees: machinists, mechanics, and their sons. He also brings his two boys, one in his early twenties and the other in his mid-teens, along with a few of their friends. So Jake is basically footing the tab for a large contingent of Midwestern factory workers who would otherwise never experience a fishing trip such as this one.

The scene this week is one you rarely see in a high-dollar fishing camp: a crew of guys with chew pushing out their bottom lips, wearing camouflage neoprenes, chucking hardware, and sucking down canned Budweiser as fast as we can supply it.

To be perfectly honest, this is not the culture with which I'm most familiar, and these guys don't practice the style of fishing that I particularly enjoy, but in some ways they are refreshing.

Often I take people fishing who are not capable of truly appreciating the experience of this place because they have the means to purchase such a trip whenever they choose. If their preconceived expectations (mostly pieced together from glossy ads and feature articles) are not met, they often leave here disappointed. Believe it or not, we can't guarantee any client a picture of himself holding a thirty-inch trout on a gravel bar pocked with grizzly prints on a bright sunny day with a moose standing majestically in the background. But that's what some people come here expecting.

In contrast, these guys are content to sit on the riverbank, drink beer, huck metal into the current, and reel in fish. They may not be the greatest sportsmen in the world—they don't really care which end of the salmon gets hooked—but they're easy to guide and they provide a dose of reality in a surreal existence.

Since the king salmon are so incredibly late this year, they can't do too much damage to our Chinook fishery—and I really don't care how many sockeyes they catch. Last year our entire sockeye run was just over a million fish, but this summer we've had over two million blow past us already. For now, the sockeye population is safe.

Jake is a salt-of-the-earth type of guy. This is a man who could buy and sell most of our clients, yet he arrived here in shoes with duct tape holding one of the soles in place. He doesn't bring big-wig captains of industry (like himself) up here to network; he brings his employees because they're the people he spends his time with. He gets a kick out of giving this sort of experience to the good people who help make him money.

He's chartered planes in past seasons to bring out cases of beer when the supplies were running low. I even heard a story about him sending out a plane with one case of whiskey on it, just because somebody in the group wanted something besides canned Bud. He's a no-bullshit kind of man. Last year, the first time I ever guided him, he hopped in the boat and said, "Okay, guy, here's the deal: you can forget to bring lunch—hell, you can even forget the rods and tackle—but if we run out of beer on the river, there'll be hell to pay."

We spent the first half of that day scouting for kings. We didn't have much luck, but after he had drained a half rack of Bud, he changed to a new game. Jake likes games. This one involved him pointing out a random braid in the river and seeing if I could drive us through it regardless of where it went. After I successfully hopped the boat over a beaver dam in a particularly narrow flow of water and safely navigated us back to the main river, he handed me a crisp hundred-dollar bill and assured me that it was not coming out of the tip he was leaving for the whole camp. I'm pretty sure he never noticed the panic thudding in my chest when we were bearing down on that beaver dam.

Jake is a very generous man, but he's not the kind of guy whose patience I wish to test. So far as I can tell, he will gladly throw down and kick the shit out of anyone standing in his way, literally or figuratively. I've heard several stories of him doing just that.

Today Jake assembled six guides and all twenty-two of his guests on the same gravel bar for an impromptu sockeye tournament. It was Jake's tournament, so everyone understood that Jake's team was going to win. Considering the prize at stake was a jar of Goober Grape (the peanut butter and jelly pre-mix), it didn't really matter anyway.

The rules were simple: there were no rules. People were throwing rocks into holes, slashing lines with pocket knives, and getting tackled into the water. It was the antithesis of the somber tone that so often accompanies the guiding that I do. No one cared or whined about catching (not catching) a big fish. There were no anal discussions or palpations about rod and reel performance or casting technique. This was all about being there and having fun. Well, that and drinking lots of beer.

At the end of the day I was running the shuttle service, ferrying all the people from the gravel bar back to camp, but Jake wasn't ready to go home. I saved him and one of his machinists for the last run, and then I sat in my boat as the evening crept in around us while they talked about life. They talked about raising kids to be tough and strong. Jake told of how he worked his way up from being on food stamps. They talked about shooting deer in their hometown, how to build the perfect shotgun, and how they struggled to prove themselves as men in the eyes of their fathers. They compared the mafia ties their grandparents each had, and they lamented the deaths of shared small-town acquaintances. They discussed what they couldn't understand about their teenage sons and the things that made them most proud of those boys.

We sat out there so long that another guide brought us paper plates heaped with steak and potatoes for dinner. I sat and listened and tried to blend into the background. I didn't want to intrude on a moment of sublime friendship. The bears wandered around us, feeding heavily in the late-day cool. I sat with a loaded shotgun across my knees, but they kept their posturing and hostilities among their own. We ran out of food and beer as the smell of rain turned into splattering drops on the river. It was time to go home.

Do I want to spend an extra four hours on the river every day? No. But it felt right today. If every group was like this, I wouldn't work here; this is not the kind of guiding I came to do. But I'd be lying if I said I didn't learn anything from these guys.

JULY 19

HIKE FOR PIKE

Roughly seven miles upstream from the lodge is a nondescript trail that branches away from the south bank and leads off into the spruce trees. If you follow the trail for about a mile, it will lead you to a pristine, glacial lake. The trail has been carved into the deep, dark soil by generations of bears, moose, and wolves.

When you emerge from the thick brush, sweating and swarmed by insects, you'll find yourself standing knee-deep in a shallow inlet choked with bright green reeds. The game trail continues out into the flooded vegetation—a trampled, matted throughway toward the open water. It's a pristine lake, hardly touched by humans, that was carved into the land by a shifting glacier during the last ice age. It's perhaps a mile across and it sits in a bowl of earth surrounded by stands of tall spruce. The lake exudes solitude, and its deep, clear water teems with hungry pike.

The pike here have little to eat, so they grow slowly. An ichthyologist-guide friend of mine estimated that a thirty-four-incher we killed and ate was probably a decade old. A big pike here is thirty-five inches or better, but the same limited food source that stunts their growth makes them willing to eat almost anything that swims by. Hiking in and fishing this lake is a nice change of pace for clients interested in a slightly different wilderness experience.

Chances of encountering wildlife at close quarters are good, and clumps of brown and blond fur cling to some of the trees along the trail. I always shoulder a loaded shotgun for this hike.

Today we had no close encounters with large mammals, but we enjoyed a spectacular afternoon. The weather was great, the lake was high, and the pike were biting as voraciously as the mosquitoes. If the tangy, orange salmon berries along the trail had been ripe, it would have been a near-perfect day.

This group of clients didn't require my constant attention, and they insisted that I fish. So while they launched spoons and spinners out across the mirrored surface, I followed behind with a sink tip and a large Clouser minnow. We caught plenty of healthy, eager pike, and the clients had a blast. But I did have one monumentally stupid moment.

One of the sports, Derrick, mentioned that he never gets video of himself on his trips. He had his wife's video camera along, and I offered to film him catching a few hammer-handle-size pike. Between fish, I put Derrick's camera in my jacket pocket for safekeeping. When a fly dropped from my fly patch, I reached down to retrieve it and dunked the pocket holding the camera. Derrick's wife had allowed him to bring it to Alaska on the condition that he take extreme care whenever using it. That was a $400 brain fart for me, and I felt like a complete jackass; a lost week of tips seemed like an appropriate penance. Derrick was cool about it and felt bad about taking the money, but he knew his wife would have his ass if he didn't.

Soon after I dunked his camera, Derrick and I saw a loon surface about thirty feet out from shore. I had heard their maniacal, laughing calls on this lake but had never seen one. When the large bird broke the surface and shook water from its inky head, we stood and gazed in amazement at its grace and bulk as it glided atop the surface, the intricate markings of true black and pure white mixed in a checkerboard pattern along its neck and wings. After regarding us momentarily with a bright red eye, the loon lunged forward and dove back under the surface to continue feeding.

I told Derrick that the loon was eating baitfish and pike were sure to be around. He made a cast just as the bird reappeared on the surface. Deciding that he needed a picture of the starkly painted loon, he pulled out his (dry) still camera just as a pike slammed into his lifeless spoon. Rather than risk missing the photo, he held the rod gingerly with one hand and focused on the loon with the other. After he got his picture, he meticulously stowed the camera and hauled back on the pike, which was still sulking and probably wondering what the hell it had just eaten. As soon as the fish felt tension, Derrick's drag screamed and his rod doubled over. A few minutes later he landed the best fish of the day: a toothy denizen that taped out close to three feet.

As we made our way back to the river, we came across the bones of what must have once been a massive moose, likely a victim of winterkill. We measured the rack at seventy inches. Derrick is a young, rather burly guy, and he decided he wanted to take the skull and antlers back to camp. I told him that he was free to do what he wanted, but I wasn't going to carry that thing back to the boat; I was content to appreciate it where it lay. Though picked clean of meat by the tundra food chain, the artifact carried a pungent funk of old rotten moose and summer swamp stench. It weighed at least eighty pounds.

With a smile on his face, Derrick shouldered it up and carried it back to the boat with greasy moose rot dripping down the back of his Simms jacket.

Underwater rainbow release

Naknek, Alaska on a waning tide

Morning fog over the river

Broken down on a gravel bar

Carpentry 101

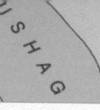

The bare essentials for 17 weeks in the bush

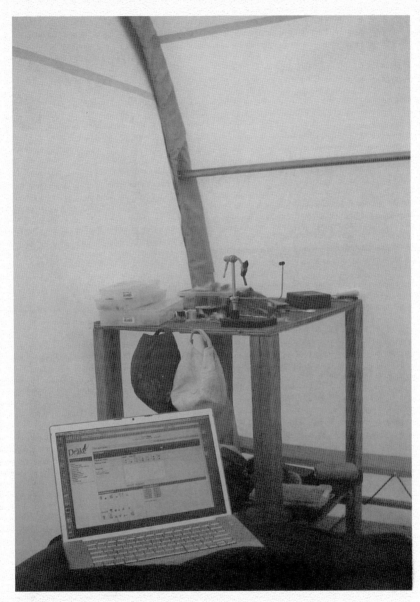

Miles' fly-tying bench, office and bedroom

A heavily spotted leopard rainbow

Char...dolly...who knows?

The "Day of Days" Fish

Releasing a 27-incher

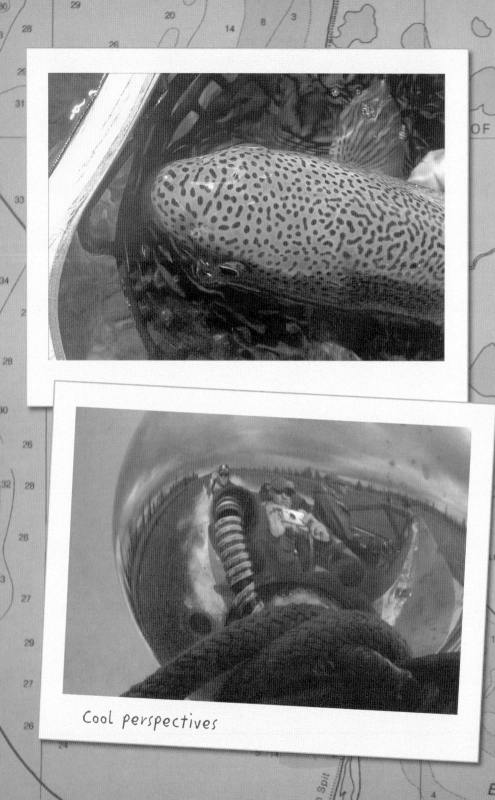

Cool perspectives

How to void a warranty on a Gore-Tex jacket

Dillis grippin' and grinnin' with a dark king

The original Alaska subsistence anglers

Prowling for salmon

Size 12 boot and a big, big bear

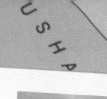

Scenes from the pike lake

Lehua fishing for spawners

Chum salmon sporting fangs

Walk softly and carry a big net

A low-maintenance client

Sockeye carnage: from the river to the skillet

Shore lunch: the best part of sockeye season

What you don't want to see when you wake up in spike camp alone with no shotgun

What happens when you unleash a flamethrower inside a Coleman Garden Gazebo

USHAGAK

An inquisitive camp visitor

Rainbows like beads

Which is the real egg?

Miles showing off the perks of spike camp

Recharging the ecosystem

The tail end of the season

Guide hands

STOLEN MOMENTS

Today I was given a reprieve from another day of dodging flying jewelry hurled by drunken salmon snaggers. The odd man out for the past few days has been a lone Cabela's employee. This man's job is to check out lodges and outfitters to see if Cabela's wants to suggest that people spend money there. Sounds like the perfect job, except he has to live in Sidney, Nebraska.

He's a perfectly nice fly-fishing industry guy who was stuck in the midst of a group with whom he did not belong. He's leaving a few days early, but not as a result of the other guests. It was scheduled that way, and today I was assigned to take him fishing downriver and then drop him off at his plane at 3:00 p.m. All of our clients arrive and depart by floatplane at a spot seventeen miles downriver from the camp. It's the closest safe place for a water landing.

He was set on trout, and the fishing was slow, but the sun was shining, and with sufficient perseverance we got into a few fish. It was one of those rare, gorgeous days; hot with just enough cloud cover to keep you from overheating and enough breeze to keep the bugs at bay without making it a chore to cast.

About 2:30 p.m. we were cruising along with a seventeen-year-old 50 hp outboard pushing us through narrow channels and across wide flats. We were two miles from the landing spot when the motor began to lose power. It sputtered for a bit, revving and faltering, before it died entirely and refused to start again. I did a quick idiot check: yes, the fuel line was still connected and, no, I wasn't standing on it. I pulled off the cowling to see if anything was obviously awry, but my superficial, nonexpert glance provided no new clues as to why the engine stubbornly refused to cooperate.

Meanwhile time was ticking by and the plane was on its way. We probably could have rowed downriver in plenty of time, but we were lacking a functional oar system. We had the oars but no oarlocks. Supposedly they were ordered two months ago . . .?

With no other options, I grabbed an oar, kneeled on the bow, and did my best Huck Finn impression. Luckily the river that far down is relatively slow and not too difficult to navigate, even with such rudimentary steerage and power.

After a mile or so, we came upon a boat from another lodge. I poled us awkwardly over to the gravel bar on which they were parked. It was an embarrassing moment, and I could see the guide stifling a smile as I limped my antique, injured craft toward him. I held my head high and shook his hand. "Hey, how's it going today?"

"Not too bad, catching a few fish."

"Listen, I need to ask a favor. I'm having some motor trouble and I've got to get this guy down to meet his plane at Hanson's by three. If you were planning on going downriver, I was wondering if you could drop him off."

"I don't know where that is. You guys have different names for spots on the river than we do."

He was not planning on making this easy for me.

"You know Hanson's, the spot just around the next couple of bends where all the rafters get picked up by the floatplanes."

"Next to that native allotment?"

"Yeah, kind of, on that gravel bar just upstream from there on the far side."

I paused and then reiterated, "Where all the floatplanes land."

"Oh, *the bluffs*. Yeah, I can drop him by *the bluffs* for you."

"Thanks, man, I really appreciate it. There's no way I would make it in time."

He nodded toward my battered boat devoid of oarlocks. "No, not with that setup."

"Yeah. Anyway, thanks."

"No problem, man. That's how it is out here—we gotta help each other out 'cause tomorrow it could be me."

He smiled a little too broadly and shook my hand again. We both knew the score. I found myself in a position of vulnerability in a place that doesn't always forgive mistakes or accidents. It was a failure on my part and he saved my ass. Fortunately, he didn't apply the barb as I was swallowing the hook. I never would have gotten my guy to the plane on time. I hope I see that particular guide in town some day; I'll buy him a beer.

We transferred the luggage from my vessel to his. I shook hands with the Cabela's guy and he climbed into the boat bearing the logo of one of our competitors. I shoved them off, and the aluminum scraping river strata sounded like a combination of mocking laughter and nails on a chalkboard. The feeling eventually faded with the whine of the outboard pushing downriver, and then I was sitting on a gravel bar . . . alone.

The river flowed steadily around me as I tried in vain to repair the deadbeat motor. I exhausted my rudimentary mechanical skills, and for the first time ever I found myself beside this meandering waterway with no impetus. There was no schedule and no way for me to get somewhere if there had been. I took a moment to relax, truly relax—the type of relaxation that's not possible for me when I have a known terminus, a fixed point at which I'll have to get back to spending my time in someone else's economy. I slumped down into one of the high-backed, padded, client seats, laced my fingers behind my greasy head, and put my wading boots up on the gunnel.

After a moment, I noticed a pod of chum salmon busting on the surface of an eddy downriver. From my nestled perch, I could plainly see their calico flanks slashing on the slack surface of the pool. I watched them a bit longer and figured I might as well catch a couple of fish while I was there. Because the trout fishing had been slow all day, I tied on a big, ugly, articulated streamer with a black magnum rabbit strip along the back and a body of palmered, pink-sparkle Estaz. It was a classic chum salmon fly if ever there was one.

Ten minutes later I was hooked up. I was expecting the rabid, reel-screaming run of the junkyard-dog salmon, not the head shakes and nimble, darting runs of a trout. The rainbow jumped and showed a gleaming stripe, bright in the sunshine, and a few moments later I had a deeply spotted trout at my feet.

Over the next hour and a half, I plied this frogwater

teeming with bright salmon and hooked trout after trout. All my instincts told me they should not have been there, nor should they have hit the fly I was throwing. Aside from that, the hole had been worked hard by the other lodge before I got here. My success was wonderfully illogical.

After landing four rainbows and losing several others, I decided to take a break and eat the last sandwich I had saved. When I opened the cooler, I discovered that my client had left behind a couple of chilly malted beverages. It was against all the rules, drinking beer on the river—and a client's beer at that. But damn it felt good to sit in that boat all alone, eat that sandwich, and drink those beers, all the while knowing that I had at least another two hours before anyone realized I was late and made the long trek downriver to find me.

I walked to the bank and decided to fish the eddy from a different angle, one that would allow me to cast at the back of the pool where most of the salmon seemed to be holding. It appeared that I had stung all the aggressive trout that were sitting on the edge of the gravel bar, so I switched to the secret weapon: a fly that I know to be deadly on aggressive salmon. It was a gigantic flash fly constructed from a generous amount of pink tinsel with a purple marabou collar and a big, red stinger hook dangling off the back. Simple but effective.

On the first cast my fly stopped dead and I was instantly into my backing. I figured I had finally found an active chum. These fish are much maligned by both sport and commercial fishermen. Their meat is not particularly sought after, and the natives prefer to dry the flesh and use it for dog food, hence the nickname "dog salmon." They're not known for their aerial acrobatics like their later-season silver cousins, so they're marginalized as bycatch rather than a targeted species. They get about the same respect as the lowly whitefish back in Montana. Similar to whitefish, chums can save a slow day by putting a bend in the rod when other species aren't cooperating, but that's where the similarity ends. Unlike whitey, a chum can reach twenty pounds, and they'll routinely bust the leaders, knuckles, and rods of unprepared anglers.

After gaining enough ground to see fly line on my spool rather than Dacron, I caught my first glimpse of the beast I was battling, and to my surprise it was another trout. A two-foot-plus rainbow that inexplicably ate the gaudiest salmon fly I had in my box. I fought him to my feet, hoping to get a photo, but he wanted no part of that plan. He flopped for a moment and then spit the flash-laden hook back at my face in disgust.

Three casts later, I finally caught my chum. A hideous, hook-jawed beast that pulled hard and swam off intolerantly when I released him, throwing a shower of water across my grin. A few casts after that I watched a big buck slam into the fly and take off downstream. For the third time in fifteen minutes I was into my backing. I gained ground on him, but he made a run for a big brush pile. I leaned back, screwed down the drag, and pulled hard—too hard. I snapped my brand new seven-weight right above the cork. The fish got away and shattered my rod in the process, but I did get my fly back as a consolation.

I spent the rest of the afternoon snoozing on the bow of the boat with a sun-faded lifejacket under my head. Around 6:30, I heard the roar of the rescue boat charging downstream. I chuckled inwardly; being lost was better than being found. Call it luck or fate, but those four hours that I spent alone were the finest hours I've had all season, or at least since my previous stranding back on Day 2.

It took another three hours and two more trips up and back to return the derelict vessel to camp. Five of us had to manually lift the boat and outboard into the hold of our landing craft and then drag it out again when we finally reached camp in the dwindling light.

My boat broke down, I snapped a brand-new rod, I didn't get out of my sweaty waders until almost 10:00 p.m., and I didn't eat dinner until well after that.

I wouldn't trade this day for any other.

JULY 22

COMING BACK AROUND, AGAIN

Everything has its price, and yesterday I discovered the price I'm paying for my splendid afternoon of fishing and relaxing. Approximately twenty-four hours ago I was in the process of cooking (heating) what appeared to be a delicious shore lunch of streamside burritos with Spanish rice, beans, chicken, beef, and a healthy serving of nacho cheese sauce to add cohesion. As I reached for another tortilla to toss on the heat, my lower back revolted and I was caught in a moment of agonizing stasis. All I could do was cringe and try to avoid any sudden movement that might exacerbate the problem. I remained in a crouch, bent over those cold tortillas that had traveled so far to get to this place. The muscles relaxed slightly after a moment, and I thought I had gotten away with just a warning. I tested my range of motion and appeared to be fine so long as I didn't bend too deeply. Whew, dodged a bullet there. Or so I thought.

About an hour later I sat down to dine on one of the hot-from-the-propane-grill burritos, and that singular act of putting my narrow ass on the gunnel of the boat was the last straw. Every muscle, tendon, and ligament around my lower five vertebrae gave me a collective middle finger and decided to mutiny.

I gave up on eating and laid myself on the bow of the

boat with my feet flat and my knees in the air, hoping to stem the tide of wrenching pain. One of our clients noticed my agony and decided to give me his two cents, which ended up being worth substantially less than that amount.

"What's wrong with you?"

"My back just seized up."

"Yeah, I get that every day of my life. You better get used to it, boy. Me, I got a disc in my back about this big." He held up two fingers with a half-inch gap between them. "Been like that ten years, but I don't let it stop me. You gotta just deal with it. If'n it gets real bad I chew a couple aspirin but usually I just grit my teeth and deal with it like a man."

This represented the least helpful piece of advice I have received at any point that I can remember. I stifled a few colorful comments, bit down hard, and peeled myself off the bow. He smirked and I kept quiet. I hobbled away and left him with his lip full of chew, his unsolicited wisdom, and his rod rigged up with a Russian river fly below a nice load of split shot: a spinning-gear version of the sockeye rig.

There were several groups having lunch together, so I got another guide to take me back to camp and look after my clients for the rest of the day. By that point, two-thirds of them were drunk and passed out on the bank anyway. I spent the ride back kneeling because I was unable to sit. Every subtle and miniscule bounce of the boat sent white-hot bolts of pain up my spine.

Back at camp, I refused a hand out of the boat and slowly picked my way up the hill to my Weatherport. I have been here ever since. I managed to make it down for dinner last night and breakfast this morning; my pride will not allow me to accept room service. The boss' wife gave me some pink happy pills

(Darvocet?), which helped a little, but I'm very bad at being injured. I'm even worse at being stuck inside this tent and marinating in my own thoughts. Worse than that, I know that my being out of commission means more work for my fellow guides and friends. They don't need this; we do enough work as it is when we have a full staff.

Here's hoping for a speedy recovery for my back and a containment of my sanity.

JULY 24

DOUBT AND SLEEPLESSNESS
IN THE NOT-SO-DARK OF NIGHT

I remain bedridden, stewing in this windowless plastic oven. It has been sunny and warm and my tent heats to an intolerable sheet-soaking temperature by early afternoon. My choice is to continue roasting myself or open the door and admit a steady stream of cool air and biting insects.

Lehua spends much of the day panting on her bed in the corner. When it gets too hot in the tent, she wanders outside and plops herself in the cool dirt beside the door. She knows that something is awry and has been doing her best to keep me company, but she dislikes heat as much as any creature I've ever known. If the thermometer reads over seventy, she becomes lethargic and seeks out shade or water.

Most days when I'm out guiding, she can wander as she pleases. On cool days she and the other camp dogs will ramble around the wilderness, following the enchanting scents that dogs seem unable to resist, or chasing local critters smaller than she is. On warm days she lies in the shade or wanders down to the dock where she waits for the migrating salmon to get too close. If they come within range, she flings herself into the river with her legs splayed and her mouth open. The sockeyes are fresh and nimble, so her success rate with them is zero. Later, when the chums begin to spawn, she'll spend most of the day on the dock with her eyes trained on their underwater procreation rituals. These fish she'll occasionally catch, drag up on shore, and abandon, her interest lying only in the catching of her prey. There the tired salmon will suffocate, fester, and become a foul-smelling mess in which Lehua will roll a few days later.

My status as temporary invalid has interrupted her schedule. I can tell that she wants to be out following her daily routine, lavishing in doggy heaven, but she seems compelled to stay with me. I appreciate the company but feel a slight twinge of guilt for taking her away from her charmed life.

I almost never have trouble sleeping. This is especially true here, where sheer exhaustion causes me to lapse into a ketamine-type slumber as soon as my head hits the pillow. The actual precipice of sleep is like water vapor or a female orgasm: amorphous and difficult to define, yet easily comprehended in theory. That is to say, you know when you find it, but how you got there is another matter.

For me, the inability to fall asleep is always the result of an overly talkative mind untempered by physical exertion. Two days in bed have put me in exactly that state. And if insomnia isn't bad enough, my isolation and boredom the past couple of days have also caused me to pine for female companionship more intensely than normal. When I find myself overagitated, I tend to write letters to ex-girlfriends. It's a habit that has gotten me into trouble in the past.

Last night, after lying awake for hours and staring at my canvas ceiling, I pulled out my laptop and poured forty-eight hours' worth of loneliness and self-loathing into my hard drive.

I wrote the first "poor me" e-mail to an ex-girlfriend

that I met when I was working in Botswana. We were close, for a while, but I haven't seen her in a long time. She just disappeared from my life, stopped returning phone calls and e-mails. I didn't hear from her for five years. One snowy day last winter she called me, startled that I still kept the same phone number. She apologized and confessed that she had freaked out. She had enrolled in an International Relations graduate program, met some guy, and moved to a small Caribbean island for a short time. She shares my wanderlust and tendency toward impulsive decisions. I don't blame her for bailing; it's something I could easily see myself doing.

Next I wrote to a woman I dated off and on for twelve years. It was a poisonous pairing that continued for about a decade longer than it should have. She now has a law degree, a fiancé, and an apartment in Los Angeles. After a year of silence, I doubt that she was just sitting around and waiting for an e-mail from her seasonally employed ex-boyfriend—but I wasn't writing it for her benefit, and I still had some juice left in my laptop battery.

I wrote furiously for several hours, transcribing pages of self-doubt, questioning decisions made, and wondering about the statute of limitations on impetuous breakups and bailouts. When my battery finally died and my screen went black, I closed the lid on my laptop and immediately fell asleep.

When I awoke this morning, I was relieved that I had written the e-mails after the generator had been shut down, cutting off the Internet connection and any chance I might have had to embarrass myself. My self-absorbed ramblings never reached their intended destination.

Spending this much time stewing in the bile that my mind produces is not healthy or productive. It leads to brain-revving. I'm not even spinning my wheels—at least that would provide a release of energy. I'm just pushing my foot to the floor without engaging the gears. In the absence of actual outlets, I'm using my energy to fuel a cancerous campaign of self-reflection and pity.

I hate drama, especially the kind that sprouts from boredom rather than actual tragedy. I need to get back to work. I need to go fishing. I need something new to write about.

JULY 31

A FAREWELL TO KINGS . . . FINALLY

I've been back in action for a few days now, my back finally coaxed into a tenuous recovery. We hired internally for the departed chef's position. One of the ladies who already works herself to death around here got the job. So now, in addition to cleaning everything and teaching afternoon school lessons to Ken's kids, she's also in charge of cooking for the entire camp. The workload hasn't changed, but now we have one less body to take care of it.

The blue-collar crew has gone, and we have moved on to a group of construction and mining executives. You would think that guys like these would bring fly rods, but these gentlemen only had two days to harass kings (Chinooks) before the season closed, and they came loaded with Shimanos and Vibraxes.

In my opinion, this lodge should not fish for king salmon. There are plenty of places in Alaska where people can fish for chrome, bright kings. We offer many fantastic fishing opportunities from this lodge, but ocean-fresh king salmon fishing is not one of them. Why promote expectations we can't meet? Oh, yeah, I forgot . . . to book trips and make money.

Given our distance from tidewater, we have two options for fishing kings. We can run a hell of a long way downriver to compete with the other lodges that are located there, or we can stay closer to home and rip fire-engine-red fish off their spawning beds. Marketing this lodge as a king hotspot is like selling adult diapers at Victoria's Secret. It just doesn't make sense.

Today marks the glorious end to our harassing these poor tired fish who just want to get laid one time before they die. Today I can say good-bye to the 5:00 a.m. downriver marathons and jockeying for position with boondoggling snaggers, back-trolling pluggers, and self-righteous fly fishermen anchored up in the middle of the run who make everyone else go around them while shooting defensive glares. Good-bye to standing on gravel bars and sight-fishing to tomato-can-red submarines with orange flies, then pink, then chartreuse, then white. And if none of those work, drifting beads over them until they either eat them or find them accidentally lodged in their mouths. Good-bye to snapped ten-weights, spooled reels, mad gravel-bar sprints, and adrenaline-stoked screams of "GET THE BOAT!" Good-bye to forty pounds of salmon flesh cartwheeling out of the water in awkward, splashy pirouettes.

Okay, I do get some enjoyment from fishing kings, but I also feel a strong guilty pang when I'm asked to fish them on their redds. Still, the excitement is hard to discount. Spawning Chinook are a vice, something you know you should ignore—but how do you ignore fifty inches of bright red fish in two feet of gin-clear water?

Now that the season is closed I can target kings for perfectly legitimate reasons. I can catch the masses of hungry rainbows that are staging behind the spawners and waiting for them to drop their eggs. Everything is fine so long as I can conjure a justification.

AUGUST 1

I'M NO CEO

It's my week for dish duty. This evening I was in the dining room refilling beverage receptacles and preparing coffee urns for the morning kick-start. The dining room (dining tent, actually) is the communal area of the camp. In a given evening, depending on the crowd, you can find people tying flies, playing cards, comparing photos, swapping stories, drinking heavily, generally unwinding, and sharing a buzz.

Bustling around after dinner, I was having a conversation with Dick when one of the clients approached. He's a nice man; I've not guided him, but he's always smiling and seems greatly appreciative of where he is and what he's doing. He extended his hand to each of us and spoke, "I just want to thank you guys for all the hard work you do here. You all go out of your way to make this a first-class experience, and I just want you to know that I recognize and appreciate it. I'm no CEO like the rest of these guys—like most of the guys you get out here. I'm a working guy, like you guys, and I know what it takes on your part."

I gave him the stock, deferential answer that I fall back on when complimented in such a way. People seem to like holding their fantasies about guiding intact, so I shook his hand and replied, "When this is your office," pointing toward the view of the river, "it's hard to complain."

He repeated his bearing and gave us a look of pure solidarity and understanding, "Work is work. I'm no CEO; I'm a working guy, like you guys."

Dick, as usual, stepped in and steered the conversation toward humor. "Work? Shit, we don't know how to do anything—and if we did, we'd suck at it." He flashed me a wink and I excused myself to go finish the dishes.

It was an interesting moment. Here's a guy who obviously has enough money to afford a trip such as this one. He brought with him a group of eight men, his friends the CEOs, yet he stood here on the other side of the room, professing the distance he felt between them and the closeness he felt toward us. There he was with the help, convening with the smelly, broke guys who live up the hill in relative squalor and use their sum total of intellect to help people fool semi-intelligent creatures into biting dressed hooks.

His appreciative compliment illuminated a trend that I've noticed among many of the men I've taken fishing. There is a desire to appear "working-class" in my presence, despite their having a decidedly upper-class income. Maybe they're seeking a status that somehow makes them more masculine, while also bridging the gap between us. As though having money and an office job makes them less manly than if they were struggling to earn a living with their backs, like me.

I don't know the man, and I don't know what he does for a living. So far as I'm concerned, we're all "working guys." Just because some guys do it in suits and others in waders doesn't change the fact that it's all work. Some jobs pay better than others and some have better fringe benefits—like my daily commute and the view from my office.

I figure I'll choose what makes me happiest and stick with it until it doesn't make me happy anymore. After that, I'll do something else.

NEVER A DULL MOMENT

As the waves of sockeyes rush upriver toward the lakes that will eventually sustain their young, their entire physiology changes. The sudden hormonal rush that these fish experience makes human puberty seem like a gradual metamorphosis.

The lead-up to sexual maturity changes everything about a salmon: their behavior, bodily function, and appearance. When they enter fresh water, they stop feeding as their bodies begin breaking down and consuming their own internal organs. Their osmal regulation, the systems used to uptake and retain water, shifts 180 degrees. Most notably for us is the drastic change in the way the fish look. The males grow large protruding humps on their backs, and their jaws elongate and sprout sharp teeth that are used for bullying and fighting during their spawning regimen. Males and females alike will darken and blush, and they'll eventually become a bloom of blood-red lingering at the mouths of feeder creeks and staining the clear, cold water. There they wait for the right amount of rainfall to coax them up the narrow trickles to begin the arduous process of spawning. They get to do this only once; it will be their last gasp (or is it a moan?).

These fish have endured. They have skirted set nets, seals, lead-slinging snaggers, and seventy miles of river current complete with boiling rapids and surging drops. Now they're making the last leg of their journey. The narrow waterways concentrate their bright red bodies so densely that the hordes of hungry brown bears will pick them off, occasionally two at a time, with explosive leaps and calculated pounces.

Today we retraced their path—not to fish for sockeyes, but to catch the large, voracious trout that assemble to gorge on their spawn. The salmon won't start digging redds in the gravel for another week. Their eggs won't show up in the water column in any significant supply for about two weeks, but the rainbows are anxious and hungry, willing to eat most anything that resembles a sockeye egg.

Like the salmon, we also have to make a harrowing journey to reach these waters. Between our lodge and the lake there are twenty miles of treacherous river with two Class III rapids and several miles of zigzagging rock garden. No other outfitter currently sends boats through this section of river, though we aren't the only ones to fish the streams that feed the lake. They're easily accessible to anyone with a floatplane. We're just the only ones crazy (stupid) enough to run clients up there by boat.

Today was our first trip up to the lake; the run is about an hour and a half from the lodge. For the person driving the aluminum v-hull with 350 horses roaring at the stern, it requires about forty minutes of intense concentration and hand-eye acuity. We encountered the first major obstacle about nine miles upriver from the lodge where the river tumbles through a lush box canyon. Eagles and ospreys nest in the crevices of the overgrown rock walls; they are unsettled observers of our battered boat as it rattles the silence of this remote place.

Here the steep canyon walls pinch the river into two

successive Class III rapids. The first is a boiling, standing wave about four feet high. Today we were properly aligned; we balanced only for a brief, gut-borrowing moment on the precipice of the surge before we crawled up and over with the engine at full scream.

Just beyond the big roller we found a straight but jarring wave train running down the center of the flow. We avoided most of the heavy water by hugging tight behind a large boulder at river right. From there, we got a good angle as we crawled past the pitches and valleys of the wave train that rolled and surged just a few feet to the side of our boat. At the top of the rapid we slipped out from behind the boulder and gunned the engine. It took all she had to push us through the remaining funnel blast of current with our full load of swollen sports, sodas, snacks, and gear.

These rapids present the highest degree of consequence if the captain makes a mistake or if we have an engine problem at the exact wrong moment. If the boat winds up sideways or loses power, the chances are good that the passengers will find themselves swimming while the boat bounces along the bottom. Fortunately, there's a nasty sweeper just below the rapids where most of the death and destruction will likely collect. Reading the line is relatively easy; as long as you don't do anything stupid, you'll make it through.

Beyond the rapids, the river widens and allows a mile of calm and ease before the next difficulty. The rock garden consists of wide, sweeping bends with a rapid descent; its numerous boulders produce a frothy, jagged nightmare. We found the channel, the safe passage, but still we were constantly darting and sliding around boulders. Some were emergent geological beasts worn smooth by centuries of flowing water. Others lurked just below the surface with only subtle current disruption. In water as angry and aerated as this, finding these sleepers can prove difficult. Even if you know the route and see all the rocks, you still have to weave through them without spinning the boat. Ken, who has twenty years experience with the route, tells everyone the same thing. "It's not a question of if you hit a rock; it's a question of when. Trust me, you're going to hit rocks. You just hope that it's a glancing blow with minimal trauma."

After three miles of white-knuckle NASCAR power sliding, the river flattens again into a long, gentle slick. Here, closer to the lake, the towering spruce trees are replaced with alders and other squat foliage. We began to see skiffs moored along the banks; they belong to fly-out lodges and we hoped their guys were not waiting for us upstream.

Without ceremony, we emerged from the river and into the lake, now contending with the bounce and roll of wind swell rather than current. We hugged the south bank and made our way to the silt-colored mouth of the tributary that we planned to fish. As the boat pulled into the small creek, stark red clouds of spawning sockeyes parted ahead of our bow and reformed in our wake. We pulled up to a riffle with an eddy deep enough to park the boat and began preparations for the afternoon. The shotgun was loaded and set aside, and then we strung the rods and loaded our packs.

For the next four hours we fished our way up a half mile or so of narrow creek bordered with thick brush. The deep, lush grass had been trampled along the banks. In the heavier thickets there were tunnels that snaked through the undergrowth. Freshly stripped sockeye carcasses and steaming piles of their digested remains littered the path.

Protocol here is to have two guides armed with shotguns. Everyone stays close together; there is no sneaking off into the woods to take a whiz. If you have to go, you turn around and do it where you stand. As our sports fished their way upstream, we spent our time acting more as bear deterrents than fishing guides.

It defies my sense of logic and self-preservation to stand my ground when an 800-pound bear charges directly at me, full tilt, and then stops not thirty feet from where I stand. It invokes my ingrained "fight or flight" response, but in this case I don't think either option would work out very well. Even though the bear is running down salmon and uninterested in me, just having such a fearsome predator barreling down on me is somewhat surreal. Even more disturbing is the fact that I have willingly put myself in this position. I often wonder what would happen if the bear changed his mind, mid-charge, and decided to make me the meal instead of the salmon. Would the short-barreled shotgun in my shaking hands be enough to stop him?

At a point today I was watching eight different bears on a 100-yard stretch of river. They would explode downstream toward us, forcing a school of staging salmon from a deep pool into the shallow water. The humped backs of the salmon were cutting hundreds of scattering v-wakes as they fled in panic. The bears always stopped short of our position, mainly because we stood our ground and enforced our boundaries, but I swear I saw a few of them give us the hairy eyeball before giving up, fishless, and slowly stalking away.

There were sows with cubs mewing at their heels. We had bears constantly roaming across the channel, not fifteen feet from us, scanning the pools of salmon and occasionally leaping in right where we were fishing. There was a constant procession plodding through the thick brush behind us, their stench usually telegraphing their presence. It's an unmistakable aroma, like a wet, mangy dog that has rolled in rotten fish.

The bear viewing was fantastic, and we had a semi-professional photographer on hand to capture some incredible shots. The trout fishing was pretty stellar, too—when the sports could avoid snagging salmon in the back or tail. Roughly half the fish we hooked had to be broken off intentionally because their struggling would arouse the attention of the hungry bears. Regardless, we caught plenty of nice fish.

Because of the skinny water and the number of hungry rainbows swishing upstream amid the salmon, we were able to sight-fish most of the trout we caught. It's hard to beat sight-fishing twenty- to twenty-eight-inch rainbows all day long—except maybe if we were casting dry flies.

At the end of it all, we still had to make the long run back to camp through the maze of rapids and boulders. The additional current pushing against the transom makes the downhill run even trickier. It was one of those days that charges you by draining you completely. A day where the fishing was only a piece of the whole experience. At one point we had clients doubled up on two-foot rainbows while a half-dozen bears fished calmly above us and the sun shone warmly through the alders.

It was a succession of moments and hours that reminded me why I do what I do.

AUGUST 7

DUMPING THE SLOP BUCKETS

The task itself sounds incredibly distasteful, but it's one of my favorite duties. Garbage, in remote Alaska, means anything you absolutely cannot use any longer for any purpose. At this lodge we have three categories. First, we have burnable garbage, which are all things that can be ignited. Toxicity levels are not a factor. We also have nonburnable, which is pretty much dominated by beverage receptacles—beer cans, soda cans, the occasional glass bottle, etc. And lastly we have organic, which is anything that resembles food, or was at one time considered food but cannot be fed to the dogs.

Burnables meet an obvious fate in a fifty-five-gallon steel drum that has been shot full of holes for better ventilation. Nonburnables get double-bagged and hauled to town by either airplane or boat. Organics get dumped into the slop buckets that reside under the sink in the kitchen and are deposited in the river at the end of each day.

We all take turns on dish duty. With four people to a dishing shift, each team works a week at a time, once every four weeks. Emptying the slop buckets is part of dish duty. The slop buckets cannot be simply dumped into the river next to the camp. This would be like putting out a chum slick from a beach resort in shark-infested waters. Bears like slop: it smells, it has calories, and it doesn't run away. Each night someone has to take a boat away from camp and deposit the contents of the buckets into the river.

Tonight, while someone else dipped a mildewed mop into grimy, grayish water, I absconded from the kitchen with two five-gallon buckets of slimy lettuce, orange peels, egg shells, chicken bones, green-blooming bread, rotten leftover salmon, and rock-hard bagels. I carried my putrid booty down the winding dirt road to the boat slough in my sandals, jeans, and a t-shirt. I pulled in the anchor, hopped in the skiff, backed out of the slough, and spun the throttle on the outboard's tiller handle.

The vast majority of the time I spend driving these boats they are loaded down with expensive clients and essential gear. Normally, I'm clad from head to toe in Gore-Tex and Polartec, shielded from the harshness of the climate and protected from extremes. Trips like the one I took tonight carry only the responsibility of safely ferrying unwanted detritus to its watery grave.

The boat jumped up to speed and planed out easily with the lack of weight; instantly I was skimming across the glassy surface. Cool evening air permeated my thin clothing, flushing out the heat of the stuffy kitchen. Insects ricocheted off my face and forced me to squint as I cut into a narrow braid and power-slid around a hairpin corner. I like to test myself on these outings, to see how skinny I can run the boat. Eventually I'll push it too far and leave it high on a gravel bar with no waders or boots, but not tonight. Tonight I dialed in each skidding turn, only clipping a few trees at the outlet into the main stem.

I pinned the bow on shore at a deep cut bank, gunned the engine to climb it high enough to hold, and then shut it off before dumping the organics into the current. Once I left the engine running, and it sucked a bunch of half-rotten carrots into the jet's intake, stranding me on the bank until I removed the rank and slimy leftovers from the grate.

After the slop was dumped and the buckets rinsed, I eased the aluminum bow off the bank and spun it in the current before leaping back up on plane and racing downriver, toward the sun that was setting over the ridgeline. A shiver ran through me as the temperature continued to drop in the fading light. I killed the throttle and spun the boat out of the main current, passing the fleet slowly so as not to wake any boats. I parked the skiff, secured the anchor, and carried the empty buckets back to the steamy warmth of the kitchen where someone else had just finished cleaning the floors.

"Hey, thanks for doing the slop buckets."

"No problem."

AUGUST 9

CAN YOU GIVE ME TWENTY FEET?

Anyone who has ever guided has at some point experienced a day that should have been absolutely epic but wasn't. The hatch of the season is coming off or the cooling water has got the big browns attacking streamers with reckless abandon. There you are, on what should be an historic day, but instead you're guiding clients whose ineptitude with a fly rod negates the incredible opportunity the river has afforded. Today was one of those days, and to have it pass by unfulfilled was a major loss.

Most fishing guides have patience; you can't do this for long without it. We're used to spending entire days, or even weeks, with novice flycasters and living vicarious thrills through their minute accomplishments. Under average fishing conditions this is no big deal, but when conditions are not average—when it's happening—an inept or dispassionate angler is tough to stomach.

This week has consisted mostly of the days I've described. The chums have just begun to dig beds, and the rainbows are stacked behind them and ravenously sucking up anything and everything that's pinkish and round. As an added bonus, the silvers showed up a couple weeks early, and they're pouring into the lower river in droves. It doesn't take much skill to catch fish in these conditions. In fact, anyone can catch fish during a week like this, but anyone with even a scrap of ability could absolutely crush them. Just get the fly into the water; you don't even have to mend. The fish are so aggressive they're hitting swinging beads just as well—sometimes better—than dead-drifted presentations. Maybe they think another fish is trying to take it away from them?

Enter today's clients, two extremely nice and completely incapable fishermen. I consider myself a patient and competent instructor, but two forces are conspiring against me: their difficulty in absorbing the concepts I'm trying to convey and my shortened capacity for patience because I can actually *see* the fish swarming in front of them.

Set aside the fact that I can't get them to cast an indicator setup more than fifteen feet; we can usually overcome that. Never mind the seven feet of slack line in every drift; I can let that go. But when I have to scream "SET!" four times before they finally react with a slow, limp flop of the rod—on the upstream side—I begin to lose patience. It's even worse when they respond with a comment like "I think that was another rock."

The good news is that they learned a lot, they had a good time, and they caught fish—rainbows and chums. We didn't even try for silvers; I'm not a glutton for punishment. But as I sit here in my tent, pounding on my keyboard in frustration and replaying the opportunities of the week, all I can think of is the number of hogs we should've stuck.

AUGUST 11–15

SPIKE CAMP

Saturday

The clients I was guiding this week were on a five-day trip rather than the normal seven, so I knew I'd be spending Saturday working around camp. I got up at my usual time, had breakfast, did the morning dishes, and had just begun to rig my boat for drift-fishing (my oarlocks finally arrived) when Ken came putting down the hill from his house in the diesel 4WD golf cart.

"We're doing a spike camp on the lower river for silvers," he announced. "You're gonna set it up. The boat leaves at eleven."

It was 9:00 a.m.

I had exactly two hours to gather all of the essential gear to run an intricate spike camp for four clients. This would have been a relatively easy task if I could have used all the gear that we have set aside for raft trips—gear that's moderately organized and in known working order. Unfortunately, there's a raft trip scheduled for next week, so all those items were off limits.

For two hours I rushed around and tried to assemble a working camp. I crawled through the dusty corners of our storage space and hauled out random pieces of tents, hoses for stoves, sleeping bags, cots that didn't quite fit together, and ActionPackers stuffed with moldy cookware. A couple of guides who weren't going downriver helped me repeatedly fill the sled of the four-wheeler with equipment and haul it to the dock.

With fifteen minutes left before departure, I haphazardly threw together a bag of personal belongings, not knowing how long I would actually be down there. I brought three pairs of socks, three layers of Capilene tops, two layers of Capilene bottoms, fleece pants, waders, boots, jacket, hat, whiskey, pillow, sleeping bag, sandals, water bottle, two books, sunglasses, fly-tying kit, boat bag, and an eight-weight rigged with a 300-grain sink tip. I forgot my shotgun, shoes, a toothbrush, and toothpaste.

At 11:15, Ken, Dan, and I roared away from the dock under sunny skies with twin 350s pushing us downriver. An hour and a half and forty some-odd miles downriver, we stopped on a large, emergent sandbar at tidewater. It was about 150 yards long and 40 yards across at its widest point. It would grow and shrink by twenty to thirty percent, depending on the tides. A small tidal lagoon separated it from the swampy shore.

They dropped me off on the sandbar with all the gear and then continued on to town for a fuel run. Within minutes of their departure I began to second-guess my hurried packing and organizing. I knew I had forgotten some essentials, but I wouldn't find out for sure until I unpacked and set up camp. I planned to flag down the boat when it returned from town later in the evening. By then I would know exactly what I needed; tomorrow, when another guide brought clients down, he could deliver the forgotten items. I wasn't yet sure what I was missing, but I could make do for one night.

As I sorted through all the gear on the sandbar, I noticed two things right away: there was no shelter of any sort from the elements, and the whole area was covered in fresh bear and wolf tracks. That was when I thought about the shotgun sitting beside my bed back at camp.

For the rest of the afternoon I busied myself erecting shelters. I assembled two spacious tents for clients and one smaller dome tent for the guides. I drove all of the available (but not required) tent stakes into the soft sand at hard angles. They wouldn't survive a severe windstorm, but they would hopefully handle the intense afternoon sea breezes.

Once the sleeping tents were set, I proceeded to the other side of the sandbar to put up the "kitchen" tent. To call it a tent is a bit of a misnomer. As labeled on the box, I was actually about to assemble a Coleman Garden Gazebo, a wispy, six-sided temporary structure of screen mesh and thin nylon meant for suburban backyard barbecues, not camping in remote Alaska.

Assembly wouldn't have taken long if I had had a copy of the instructions and an engineering degree. What I did have was a collection of poles, connectors, and fabric that would require three hours and a lot of swearing and tossing of objects to erect. All six corners were affixed to the ground with eight-inch yellow plastic stakes. Read that again: six eight-inch plastic stakes. These tiny stakes, pushed into fine grains of sand, were the only things holding the giant nylon parachute to the ground on an unsheltered river bar beside Bristol Bay.

Just about the time I finished with the "kitchen," the boat returned from town. I had not had time to try out all my gear, but I'd done a quick inventory and it seemed like I was in good shape. While I had the help, the three of us retrieved a boat that the lodge keeps on the lower river. It's a battered aluminum husk that sits upside down eleven months of the year acting as a home for rodents. We towed it back to the sandbar, washed it down, put an ancient thirty-horse prop on it, fired it up, and called it good. I now had a boat and a camp. They waved good-bye and left me on the beach, carrying away my request for a shotgun, a toothbrush, shoes, sleeping pads, pillows (for clients), and beer (for me).

I wanted to fish. There were salmon busting all around my campsite, but I knew that clients were coming out the next day and I had to be prepared. I buckled down and forced myself to get everything ready before wetting a line.

Once the beds were made and the kitchen tent organized, I strung up my rod and waded out to the top of the sandbar to work the nervous water at the drop-off. Within ten casts I was locked into nine pounds of anadromous silver muscle that rocketed from the surface with a shower of glinting light. With such an auspicious start, I thought I was in for a great evening, but that was the only coho that I caught. I did catch a half-dozen hard-pulling chums, which kept me amused and routinely took me into my backing. At that point it really didn't matter; I had managed to catch myself a fantastic dinner.

Aggravated rumbles in my stomach eventually pulled me away from the meandering current and out of my sandy waders. The foam sandals I had brought were not appropriate footwear for deep sand; this was when I thought about my boots sitting under my bed. My socks became thoroughly gritty and stayed that way.

When I started to assemble the stove, I found another unpleasant oversight in my hurried packing. The hose that I brought to connect the propane tank to the burner didn't fit. The valve that should have connected to the stove was completely wrong. I fooled with it for half an hour, realized it was pointless, and started a fire. This was not the end of the world, I figured. As long as it didn't start raining, I would have no trouble cooking for my clients over an open fire.

Stuffed on fresh salmon, I settled down with a bottle of whiskey and a good book to enjoy the sunset on my island. Not perfect, but a damn good place to be. I slept well, listening to the sound of splashing fish, and woke only once to fend off what sounded like encroaching bears.

Sunday

I slept in a little, knowing that the clients wouldn't arrive until noon at the earliest. For breakfast I ate a peanut butter and jelly sandwich on wheat and skipped coffee, saving the limited wood for later meals.

I wanted the fishing to be fresh for the clients, but I couldn't resist throwing a few casts before they arrived. In the shallows, just thirty feet from me, I saw a dark shape slowing working its way upstream. I cast above and just left of it so that the bright pink fly swung right in front of the fish. The salmon hit hard and broke water immediately, beating my knuckles as it tore downstream. Once I subdued the splashing beast at my feet, I was surprised to discover that it was a bright, chrome chum. It occurred to me then that if you can't tell the difference until the fish is in hand, it doesn't really matter the species—unless, of course, you're fishing for dinner.

After a great fight with that sea-fresh chum, I forced myself out of the river and walked back to camp. Sore-mouthing the aggressive fish before the sports showed up would only come back to bite me in the ass later.

As I sat in the kitchen tent devouring a book, I noticed that the wind was beginning to pick up and blow in off the bay. Before I could react, the entire Garden Gazebo was airborne and cartwheeling down the beach. I caught it before it reached the river, but it was all I could do to walk it back into the gusting wind. As I struggled back toward camp with it, I noticed how odd the campsite looked with no tent covering the collection of boxes and chairs arranged in a circle around a table covered in cooking supplies—an insular grouping of domestic items sitting on a sandbar in the middle of an undomesticated place.

Eventually I gave up on moving the tent back to its original spot. Once I got it righted with the toy stakes back in the sand, I would rush off, between gusts, and grab a heavy object to place over each stake and on top of the fabric at each corner. The propane tank, water coolers, and soaked logs were successful at keeping the tent in place, but it still listed intensely eastward and remained under constant structural strain. Eventually all the zippers on the three doors tore apart, leaving it less than bug-proof.

Just past 1:00 p.m. four jovial clients arrived along with my friend Paul. He's an experienced guide and a seasoned outdoorsman; I was glad he had been sent down. Paul brought my shotgun and the sleeping pads—but no pillows, beer, toothbrush, or toothpaste. Oh well. My mouth was getting a little rank, but at least we could keep the bears at bay.

We had a wonderful afternoon catching salmon. For dinner we cooked a fresh coho and followed it up with beef stroganoff. The clients, well fed and buzzing with a few cocktails, convinced us to fish with them after dinner.

We finished the day lined up on the sandbar, catching salmon in the copper light.

Monday

The smell of bacon sizzling over an open fire is one of my top-ten favorite scents. Paul had also brought down some fresh biscuits and fruit from camp. Those are treats any day in this part of the world, but they're especially grand when served in a tent on a sandbar next to a river choked with salmon.

One of the clients had carried a bag of real coffee all the way from Atlanta in his luggage, and he was kind enough to share with the group. It was the best cup I'd had all summer. My boss, unfortunately, buys the cheapest brand of bulk-grind available. One day I offhandedly suggested that the clients might like a decent cup of coffee, and he launched into a tirade.

"Expensive coffee is the biggest rip-off on the face of the planet. Half of it gets poured down the drain anyway; it's like watching people pour out my money. I just can't stand it. Don't even start on the coffee thing."

I never did again. I should point out that Ken is not a coffee drinker.

A cold, clear dawn quickly turned to a blazing hot morning, and the fishing was not what it had been the previous days. Four capable anglers worked our sandbar hard and didn't land a single silver, though they hooked a few.

After lunch Paul took the group and left for camp. His plan was to fish his way back and look for active strikers in the holding water upstream. I was again left to my own devices and spent the day trying to keep the kitchen tent from flying away while alternately reading and fruitlessly casting.

In the evening the wind died, and I cooked myself a burger and watched the sunset until the swarm of biting insects became too intense for me to ignore. The bugs are bad enough at the lodge, but in the swampy tidal regions they're a force to be feared. Safely zipped into my tent, I listened to the incessant whine of beating wings. In the morning there were literally thousands roosting between the rain fly and the tent.

Tuesday

Pattering rain against nylon woke me. The taste in my mouth had become a sour, fuzzy paste that no amount of water or Altoids could remove. This group of clients would be coming down earlier, so I was up just after dawn making sure that the camp was ready. The rain was the steady, coastal variety—not enough intensity to soak you instantly, but over time the moisture can work its way through even the most impervious materials.

The boat and crew arrived before 9:00 a.m. They quickly deposited clients and headed to town for another fuel load. The water is dropping so fast in the river that we're trying to get all our fuel in before it becomes too shallow to run the big boat.

Along with the pleasant company of clients, the boat brought down an unwelcome assistant: Dan. I was already a little down about the weather and the poor fishing, but my heart sank when I saw him step out onto the sand. I knew right then that I'd be better off running the camp alone.

As unhappy as I was to see him, he did bring down a few items that I desperately needed. I was glad to finally have some beer and a gas hose for the stove; I was utterly elated to see my toothbrush.

While Dan got the clients rigged and ready for fishing, I set to work on the stove. The hose had the proper fitting to allow fuel to flow from the propane tank, but the threads to secure it to the stove were the wrong size and wouldn't bite. Using electrical tape, I devised what I thought was a workable connection. I was finally able to get the burner lit, though it didn't have much intensity. After a couple of minutes a strong gust of wind came through and ignited the gas that was leaking from my jury-rigged connection. The resulting combustion forced the hose free from the stove and created a raging flamethrower. The hose snaked back and forth in the air like a Water Wiggle, one of those lawn toys attached to a garden spigot that I played with as a kid—only this one was spewing flame rather than water. I shut the valve off at the tank but not before it had melted a large hole in one of the screen walls of the kitchen tent. The stove was once again out of service.

Later I left Dan at camp and went in search of aggressive salmon with the clients. While I was trying not to burn down the kitchen, they had landed only one silver from our sandbar. I left Dan a list of duties that needed to be accomplished by the time I returned, the most important being a cooking fire. I knew this was a tall order in the rain, but there was abundant paper and wood—plus we had gasoline. Anyone can make fire with those ingredients, right?

Fishing was slow for silvers, but we got a few, and the chums did their part to keep rods bent. When we arrived back at camp four hours later, Dan had indeed built a fire, and he had also filleted the one fish. That was it. That was four hours. At least he recognized his priorities. While I set about the task of preparing dinner and serving the clients, Dan sat on his ass, drank beer, and threatened to gather firewood. When dinner was finished, he got up and proclaimed that he was going to gather all the wood we would need for the next day, but he apparently got sidetracked en route and wound up standing in the river fishing while I did the dishes.

After the kitchen was closed, we sat around with the clients, poked at the damp embers in the fire, and talked as the sky slowly darkened. Near eleven, I retired to bed and left Dan alone with the fire.

Around 3:00 a.m. I was jolted awake by the weight of someone falling on me and scrambling around in the tent.

"What the hell are you doing? Your bed's over there."

In a drunken stupor, Dan had climbed into the back flap of the tent where I was sleeping and tripped over me.

"Oh sorry, dude. I was . . . uh, shit. There was this bear out there and I scared him off 'cause I heard him in camp, but I scared him off."

He apparently figured, since I was already awake, that now was a good time to talk. "I got plenty of coals going, so there'll be coals in the morning. I got us coals, dude. We got coals, so the morning fire should be good to go. 'Cause I got coals."

I guess he finally tired of talking about coals and my not answering because he eventually went to sleep.

Wednesday

At 5:30 a.m. I awoke. It took me a minute to realize why I was no longer asleep; I'm not one to wake undisturbed at that hour of the morning. My alarm hadn't gone off, but I could hear the drone of mosquitoes buzzing all around. Within a few seconds I began to feel intense burning and itching on most of my exposed surfaces. I figured Dan must have let a bunch of bugs in the night before and they had been feasting on me all night. The alarm would go off in half an hour anyway, so I decided I might as well get up. Upon rising, I discovered that the back flap was wide open and the tent was swarming with mosquitoes. He hadn't even bothered to zip it shut last night; he just opened it and fell in. Bug-bitten, tired, and pissed off, I climbed out of my sleeping bag, hoping he was also covered in welts.

I told him it was time to start breakfast as I left the tent. He groaned, rolled over, and said he'd be right there. The rain had ceased sometime in the night, leaving behind soggy sand and broken clouds.

At 8:30, when Dan finally did decide to get out of bed, I had built a fire, brewed coffee, cooked breakfast, fed the clients, and was just about to start the dishes. He looked at me bleary-eyed and asked if there was any coffee. I didn't answer; I just continued toward the river as though I hadn't heard him. I knew that if I said anything, I'd snap and it would be an ugly, public scene.

Rather than risk having him sit on his ass all morning and do nothing, I informed him that he would be guiding the first shift while I worked in camp. He knew better than to protest, but he shot me an irritated glance.

Thick with gloom, I went about the tasks of the day, cleaning mounds of moist grit from tent floors, turning out cots and sleeping bags, organizing the food, and making lunch. When the group returned to eat, they had caught only one silver, and I realized that I hadn't heard any fish crashing the surface in a while. I decided that we would need to look upriver if we hoped to get consistent hookups. Apparently there had been very few new arrivals on the recent tides.

We all went upriver together for the afternoon session.

I drove the boat as we searched all the best sloughs, finding nothing but chums. These guys were tired of chums, a fact they made abundantly clear. At one point, while the backing was peeling off one man's reel, his jubilation turned to dejection when we saw the massive hook-jawed chum break water. "It's just another dog," he muttered with disdain. It blew my mind when he started tight-lining the fish and trying to break it off. No, it wasn't the silver he wanted, but it was still a beautiful, strong-fighting salmon.

Three miles and nearly as many hours later, the situation was starting to get desperate. The clients were tired and annoyed and I needed to make something happen—fast. By sheer luck, I pulled up to a slack-water bar that I had never fished and had never seen anyone else fish. I climbed the high bank and saw a sizable number of silvers milling among the knot of spawning chums. Just as I was walking the skiff into casting range, one of our bigger boats came ripping around the corner to pick us up. It was the boss with his family in tow; they had come to haul the clients and me back to the lodge.

Ken explained that Dan was staying behind to tend the spike camp. It had been decided that he would cause the least amount of harm if he was isolated on a small sandbar. We wouldn't be sending any more clients down there until next week, and we needed someone to make sure that all our gear wasn't stolen or destroyed by bears.

I climbed onboard with the boss, leaving the clients in the skiff with Dan to fish while we ran back down to the spike camp to retrieve everyone's personal gear. As we pulled away, one of the guys locked into a nice buck silver. I breathed a sigh of relief. We had pulled it off and tonight I'll be sleeping back in my Weatherport.

That one spot made all the difference. On the ride back to the lodge, they raved to the boss about what a good time they had had and my abilities as a guide. Had we not stumbled upon that hole, none of that would have been said. The trip upriver would have been sullen and heavy with disgruntled silence. Instead, they toasted me from their hip flasks, slapped my leg, and laughed whiskey breath in my face. Arbitrary praise.

Lehua lavished me with sloppy, wet appreciation upon my return. She wriggled between the legs of my waders and flopped onto her back, making sure I didn't neglect the belly scratch. My hard bed has never felt so wonderfully good. I'll be able to enjoy it for the next few days and then I'm scheduled to guide a week-long raft trip. After the spike camp fiasco, I can't say that I am brimming with excitement. Luckily Dan won't be involved.

AUGUST 20-26

RAFT TRIPS ARE A PAIN IN THE ASS

In theory, raft trips seem so idyllic: floating serenely down a wild and scenic waterway unencumbered by the messy noise of a petroleum-burning engine. I also like the idea of self-sufficiency—having all of your necessities with you as you float downriver from spot to spot. It's like a wilderness backpacking trip, only with several hundred pounds of manufactured gear and packaged food.

To find a beautiful spot at which to erect temporary shelter; to catch a few fish and have a hearty, rustic meal; to sit around a fire, share laughter and a bottle of whiskey; to ultimately retire under a dry tent set atop a flat piece of soft ground—it sounds like a lovely way to spend a week in the wilds of Alaska. Unfortunately, guiding a raft trip does not even vaguely resemble that experience.

My daily duties include getting up at dawn to start coffee and breakfast, serving the clients, clearing plates, washing dishes, making lunch, packing coolers, organizing the kitchen, breaking down camp, packing the rafts, rowing and guiding for five to six hours, finding a campsite that all can agree upon (plenty of fishable water nearby, flat ground, no rotting salmon, a fire pit . . .), unloading the boats, setting up the tents, setting up the kitchen, cooking dinner, serving the clients, doing the dishes, making more coffee and tea, serving dessert, doing more dishes, and then crawling away for a few hours of sleep on a rocky gravel bar buffered by a thin Therm-a-Rest pad because the clients get the cots.

Sounds like fun, doesn't it?

Then there are the clients. People who book raft trips usually fall into one of two categories. The first group really loves outdoor adventure, and they're genuinely excited about the whole experience of roughing it on the river. Alternatively, there are the clients who really wanted a lodge trip but didn't want to pay for one, so they now want everything they would have gotten in a lodge environment without the resources or staff to provide it. Most people fall into the latter category; the guys we had this week were a mixture of both.

It always interests me to learn of the connections that bind together fishing partners. Up here, it's mainly familial ties: usually fathers and sons (or sons-in-law) and the occasional married couple. If not related by blood, the people who come here are often colleagues. They work in the same industry or business with similar income levels that afford them this type of experience.

The four clients on my raft trip this week are drinking buddies. They know one another because they are all regulars at the same pub in Gilford, England. I can only assume that this trip was hatched during a night of copious libations. Someone suggested they all book a trip somewhere together, maybe fishing, and over the course of a few more rounds they settled on a wilderness raft trip in Alaska. I'll bet that at least one of them regretted that decision when he sobered up—but didn't want to back out.

These guys represented a diversity of dispositions and a cross section of British society. We had Royce, the retired carpenter, a man in his sixties who would have been happy to sit with a cane pole in the same spot all day, not catching fish, drinking booze and tea, and eating canned chili. Unfortunately, giving him a fly rod didn't extend the distance of his cast much beyond the length of a cane pole. He was placidly content to sit in the raft all day while chatting and taking in the scenery. His body was well worn, tired from a life of stooping and working on his feet. Sitting on unstable floating platforms for long periods can be murderous on the spine. Though he never grumbled about it, you could see that he was hurting as the week wore on. On our final day he was having difficulty getting in and out of the raft. He was the only one of the group who had not yet landed a silver, so we fished hard from the raft all day. In the afternoon he couldn't even bring himself to stand up while casting; he stayed in the padded bow seat and gritted his teeth, whipping a heavy fly rod back and forth. If toughness and determination were the forces that combined to make fly line cut through the air, this man would have been firing perfect loops across the river. Unfortunately, they carried his fly only about twice the length of his rod—too short a distance to fool a sulking salmon. At the end of that final evening, after not catching a single bloody fish, he turned to me with a big, tired grin. "I've about had enough; I believe we've both earned a drink."

Evan is a young, well-educated, jolly chap who gave up his career in the stock market, moved away from London, and now builds private ponds and lakes in the countryside. His wit and upbeat nature couldn't be dampened by the most persistent downpour. Each morning he would wake the others with a rousing version of the Seven Dwarf's theme song, "Hi-ho, Hi-ho, It's off to work we go . . ." His lyrics, however, were the words "butt ball" sung over and over again. I never caught the full detail of how the song came about, but apparently Evan found a small plastic ball in one of his hotel rooms in either Anchorage or King Salmon. When he showed it to the others in the group, they teased him that he was fondling someone's used anal bead. No matter how grumpy you feel first thing in the morning, it's nearly impossible to avoid smiling when you hear four British men singing "Butt Ball" in near perfect harmony.

James is a young man (early thirties) and a prince—actual royalty. He is the prince of a small province near Gilford. I never understood exactly what James did for a living, but I know he worked in real estate. He had recently returned from doing some relief work in northern Africa. He spoke about his doctor friends and the great work they were doing, but I never quite figured out his function there. He's handsome and extremely charismatic and obviously accustomed to getting what he wants from people without appearing pushy. He spent a good hour one day regaling me with stories of Internet dating conquests and explaining to me the benefits I might get from joining Match.com while living in Alaska.

"You could line up a whole string of birds and have 'em waiting for you when you got back." He then offered to send me a link to his profile so I could check it out and see how to get the best results.

Finally there was Brian, who deals in gems and precious metals and travels extensively around the world. He has a taste for the finer things in life (all of his fishing gear bore the Hardy label), including food. Gourmet cuisine is difficult to pull off on a raft trip in the middle of nowhere. By Day 2 Brian's enthusiasm for raft-trip fare had begun to wane. By Day 4 he was loudly lamenting the fact that he was supposed to spend this week with a lady friend on a private island off the coast of Spain, but instead he was sleeping in a damp tent beside a snoring fishing partner. Brian is an interesting sort of fellow: high maintenance but self-aware at the same time. Sure, he was a pain in the ass with endless, unrealistic expectations, but at least he knew that and didn't seem to mind that his friends enjoyed busting his balls about his dainty proclivities.

What they lacked in fishing experience or knowledge of the outdoors, they made up for in alcohol consumption. No matter what the day was like—slow fishing, drizzling rain, a less than ideal campsite—they were always willing to dig into the liquor stash early and often to keep things moving. They had brought with them seven cases of beer, three bottles of whiskey, two bottles of brandy, and nine bottles of wine for an eight-day raft trip. They drank it all; I was impressed.

Laughter flowed with us along our entire twenty-eight-mile journey. I heard more foul language this week than even I'm accustomed to, and I live in a tent camp with a bunch of dudes. For the most part it was a pleasant trip, but Brian was difficult to please, and he promoted a grass-is-always-greener mentality among the group. If they were catching trout, they wanted silvers; once we passed the trout water to chase silvers downstream, they wished we had spent more time catching trout.

Brian's eating habits turned out to be the major challenge of the week. He wouldn't eat carbs or chicken, a fact that we didn't discover until we were already on the river with the meals packed in coolers. This is a tough order to fill when all your lunches are sandwiches and all your dinners involve chicken, pasta, potatoes, or bread. On the first night he came into the kitchen tent while Paul and I were preparing dinner.

"So, what are we having tonight, then?" he asked

nonchalantly, while skeptically studying the sizzling pans and boiling pots.

"Spaghetti and meatballs with fresh-baked garlic bread," I answered.

He made a hissing sound as he sucked through his teeth. "Yeah, I guess I'll just have some sauce and meatballs, then—you do know that I'm not eating any carbs."

"Well, we can try to put together something else," Paul said, "but we don't carry a lot of spare food with us."

We made special meals for him, most of which he turned up his nose at. He would eat a few bites and throw the rest in the river. After returning from depositing his dinner with the fish, Paul or I would ask if he had gotten enough and if the food was alright.

"It was fine," he responded after one of the meals he had thrown away. "I'd rather drink my dinner, anyway."

The real highlights of this raft trip occurred after dinner. They insisted upon having a campfire of epic proportions—nightly. To ensure that we would have enough wood, we stopped during the day anywhere we saw thick pilings of dry logs and stacked them atop the heavily laden rafts. As the wood burned down to soft glowing embers in the cool dark, we played trivia games that I can only assume were favorites at their shared pub. What began the first night as a way of passing time and getting to know one another had transformed by week's end into a raucous spectacle.

The game was relatively simple: first a category was chosen. We began with names of bands and progressed as far as nonmotorized tools. The first person calls out a name or item within the category and the next person in the circle then has to say a different name or item that begins with the letter that ended the name of the previous answer. So if I were to say "Oingo Boingo," the person next to me would say "Ozzy Osbourne" or any other artist or band whose name begins with an *O*.

By the end of the week the game had turned into something altogether different. Standard practice on our raft trips is to heat volcanic river rocks in the fire and then use them as foot warmers in our sleeping bags on cold nights. One evening, Paul pulled one out of the fire, cooled it slightly in the river, and then passed it between his hands like a hot potato, thus sparking a new incarnation of the game. In this improved (and vastly more amusing) version, each contestant had to come up with his trivia answer while juggling a searing-hot river rock. This made conjuring up the name of a nonmotorized tool that begins with an *R* a little more challenging. On the last night (and I must admit I'm a little fuzzy on how this actually came about) we gave up on the game and laughed ourselves silly watching Paul dance and whoop frantically as he tried to shake a hot rock out of his pants. I feel the need to note that Paul willing placed the searing rock there.

Though we laughed and enjoyed ourselves with these guys, the fact remained that we were constantly at their beck and call. This is the nature of the client-guide relationship. Regardless of what shared experiences brought us together, I was always guiding and never truly relaxing. They were spending their money; I was making mine.

I think I would have been much better equipped to handle this trip earlier in the season. I'm getting burned out. We have reached that point where I can see the end but can't quite touch it. Three weeks to go and I have officially pegged my fun meter. Eight straight days of going nonstop from 7:00 a.m. to 11:00 p.m. has sapped my remaining energy. I know there is a store of fourth wind hidden somewhere within me, but I just can't seem to conceptualize it tonight. My sails are flaccid. Right now all I know is this: I have never been so happy to be back in camp, take a shower, and eat a meal prepared by someone else. Over the past two weeks I have spent three days in my own tent. I'm ready to be a lodge guide again and then go home.

Twenty-one days and counting.

AUGUST 27

ON SECOND THOUGHT,
I LIKE BEING A FISHING GUIDE

Blessed is a boat with a motor and a short, ten-hour workday. The wind howled today. It was a downriver gale that knocked down casts and tore off caps. I took out a fellow guide that I know from Montana who brought up a group of clients from the lodge where he works. He and one of his sports, both talented sticks, worked hard all day in the blasting wind for a decent number of smaller fish. We didn't break twenty-two inches, but the sun shone bright as I walked the skiff down braids and channels, giving advice, and netting fish.

I enjoy watching someone approach a run and helping them understand the concepts of where the fish are lying and what they're eating. I get a vicarious thrill when they start dropping casts and throwing mends in the places that I would. I grin right along with them from the backside of their camera while I'm photographing their proud moments. I share their feeling of accomplishment when we release their fish and watch it descend back into the river.

AUGUST 28

THE KIND OF DAY I DREAM ABOUT

The wind blew itself out overnight and swept away all remnants of moisture in the sky. It was thirty degrees in my Weatherport when I awoke, a sure sign of a clear day to come. This time of year we're losing five minutes of light every day. I get to see sunrises now—golden orange reminders that I have another day to breathe in this air and float on this water.

Sitting in my boat at 8:00 a.m., warming up the engine and organizing my gear, I knew that I was starting ahead of the game. I had my guide friend Pete and one of his clients that I've fished with before. He's as good a fisherman as he is a boat companion. They both had high expectations, but today I knew we could meet them. It was one of those days when I could feel it: that enigmatic confidence that accompanies success on the river.

This is one of those "make it happen" kind of weeks. These guys all own a private lodge on the Bighorn River in Montana. Pete is the caretaker and guide. They have money and they like to spend it on fishing trips. If this week goes well, they'll be booking at least one full week each year with us. Today I knew that I would have little problem making it happen. My confidence was fortified by our getting to fish the hottest stretch on the river:

a run with wide, even gravel flats full of spawning kings and the trout that have begun to key on them.

Our beat started five miles down from camp. The fishing can be a little slow on cold mornings, so we decided to drift our way down and hopefully pick up a few rainbows along the way. Within minutes we were into a cartwheeling double, and my clients tossed good-natured competitive banter over my head as I rowed the heavy skiff between the rocks.

By the time we reached our assigned water, it was 10:30 and we had already boated at least twenty nice fish. I set the guys free on the flats where they fished behind pods of spawning red submarines, plucking trout from the river by the dozens. Kevin, one of the owners, was as much fun as I remembered. We fished together last Thanksgiving when I visited their lodge on the Big-horn. This morning he brought a pair of brand new Scott rods that he insisted I fish for a bit. I made about a dozen casts and caught three trout, only one of which was less than twenty inches.

Pete brought a two-handed five-weight rod and proceeded to rake the gravel flats from top to bottom. He caught so many trout that he finally switched to a mouse fly because catching fish with the egg was too easy. The mouse didn't produce like the bead rig, but he gladly traded numbers for the excitement of big trout chasing the furry wake and engulfing the mouse fly on the surface.

Nobody kept an actual count, but I'm guessing they landed at least 150 rainbows, many of them over twenty inches. We didn't get any monsters, but we had a few shots and brought a couple to hand that pushed the twenty-five mark. It was one of those days that people refer to when they talk about fishing Alaska late in the season. As an added bonus we had beautiful weather instead of pissing rain, cold, and gray.

As I lie here on my bed recounting a phenomenal day, I can feel the ache in my legs from walking the boat down miles of deep current and running between their bent rods with my net. I'll sleep well tonight, and I'll probably wake in the morning with this stupid grin still pasted across my face.

AUGUST 29

WHAT A DIFFERENCE A DAY MAKES

Today I fished the same water with the same tactics in the same weather as yesterday with dramatically different results. We had a shitty day. Shitty only in comparison to what it was yesterday, but still a major disappointment.

I was assigned different sports. The boss had heard about yesterday's pillaging, so he set me up with the two head honchos of the group. I hate being put in that position as a guide—the "you should have been here yesterday" position. It was inexplicable; we should have had a comparable day. I put them in the right places and tied on the right patterns, but the fish just wouldn't cooperate today. My sports were not impressed, so I ran around scratching my head and trying not to vocalize my frustration.

To wrap up my really crappy day, I just learned that I'm going back to spike camp tomorrow. I nearly screamed at my boss when he told me, but then I found out that I was requested. He wasn't just trying to make me perpetually miserable.

So who knows when I'll be back to my Weatherport again? For now, just picture me sleeping on a sandbar, cooking meals in a hunched-over position, and trying to remain on the bright side.

Two weeks and three days left.

SEPTEMBER 2

PERSEVERANCE AND POSITIVITY

Well, let's just say that at least I'm persevering in my attempts to remain positive. Spike camp, though not where I wanted to be, was actually a good experience. I guided a father and his grown son, who were a lot of fun to have in the boat. We drifted our way to the lower river, and most of the first day was spent bathed in sunshine that reflected off perpetually bent rods. The trout fishing was so good that we skipped silvers and focused on rainbows until we arrived at the campsite around dinnertime.

I knew what kind of evening was in store when they pulled out the gallon of Maker's Mark and two bottles of wine. We ate beef stroganoff heated over a (working) propane stove and drank ourselves content beside a roaring fire. Driftwood burns well when sufficiently dried. There are caches of it all over the lower river, spindly knots of smooth, worn stumps and branches that have drifted aground on the gravel bars and river bends.

We were a little late getting out the next morning; I may have overindulged a bit. From 9:30 to 11:00 we had residual fog and morning clouds that kept the silvers active. The moment the sun came out they developed a severe case of lockjaw. I was working my ass off trying to find a spot with some active fish when the father took me aside and said, "Look, I don't particularly like fishing for salmon—I'm doing this for my son. We've caught some fish and he's happy; let's go back to camp for lunch and a nap." I was more than happy to oblige.

When our reinforcements arrived that evening, I was informed that we would be removing the spike camp. Although it was a bitch to take down the camp, I reveled in the work. I took great satisfaction in knowing that I would no longer be sent to that bug-infested sandpit to cook, clean, and guide for sixteen hours a day.

We burned the Garden Gazebo before we left.

It was glorious.

SEPTEMBER 3

WHY I HATE COMPOSTING TOILETS

We have a fellow from Orvis in camp this week. I guess he's here to check out our operation and decide if we get the gold star of approval. I know this particular individual, and he is a very nice guy. I was supposed to take him fishing today, just him and me. I was hoping to show him around the river, enjoy the warm weather we've been having, and catch some fish—a pressure-free day. That was the plan last night, anyway.

When the guide schedule was concocted, it was forgotten that one of our boats shit the bed last week, so today the Orvis guy got lumped into another boat and I got left in camp with no one to guide.

A day in camp is not to be confused with a day off. Camp days aren't as mentally taxing as guide days; you don't have to be "on" all the time, but it's a work day nonetheless. I was given a list of tasks to complete in the morning and then left to finish them. Mostly kinesthetic work that involved hauling and lifting things: setting up a raft in place of the ailing jet boat, filling the generator, building some removable benches, things of that nature. Oh, and then there was the pinnacle of my task list, the cushy job that I saved for last. I was told to empty the tray at the bottom of the composting toilet.

In theory, I love the composting toilet. Rather than filling the ground with massive pits of human waste, we recycle our droppings back into healthy earth. It all sounds so friendly and green, like you crap into this big plastic box, turn the lever a few times, and clean dirt comes out the other side. Unfortunately, that is not the case.

Part of our problem stems from the fact that up to six clients are using a composting toilet that is "for weekend use only for three individuals." It says so on the first page of the directions. But then again, we also have a gas fireplace inside our dining room with massive red lettering that warns, "FOR OUTDOOR USE ONLY." At this camp we don't trouble ourselves with petty safety precautions or usage advisories; our motto is "make it work."

Another problem that we have with the eco-crapper is a lack of the key ingredient that actually makes it work. We ran out of the composting accelerator mix about two months ago. Who knew that one five-pound bag wouldn't last through a four-month season of extreme overuse? Lately we've been dropping handfuls of tundra into the pot and hoping for the best.

The last variable that's hindering the success of our composting toilet is that urine is sterile and kills some of the bacteria that break down the waste. Despite abundant signage, guests continue to whiz in there. But, then again, we sometimes have guests who like to shit in the shower. Do people leave their sense of common decency at home when they go on vacation?

The toilet itself is a large plastic throne with a handle protruding off one side. Contained within this marvel of hardened petroleum distillate is a plastic drum attached to the handle. After dropping one's dunnage, one simply adds some more organic compound (tundra) and turns the handle a few cranks to aerate the mixture. At the bottom is a drawer that collects all the liquid that makes its way down through the drum.

For my last duty today, I had planned to carry the drawer up the hill, dig a hole, bury the contents, and collect some more "organic compound." As I approached the little shack housing the toilet, I met Lisa, one of the ladies who works around camp. Her expression told me something was terribly amiss.

"I have to tell you something, but I still want you to be my friend afterwards."

"Uh . . . okay."

"There's a big mess in that toilet for you. I'm sorry."

Without another word she turned and hurried away with a bundle of dirty laundry balled against her chest. I hung my head and marched toward my fate.

What happened, apparently, was this: someone didn't realign the hole in the drum with the hole in the toilet when they were finished, and then someone else didn't notice this before they made their deposit and spun the handle. This created a massive fecal smear around the entire outer circumference of the drum with the smashed remnants piled in the drawer underneath. I gagged and quickly exited the shack.

I don't have a weak stomach. I can handle blood and gore with no problem and vomit hardly phases me, but fresh human feces in close quarters make my stomach turn. I took a few deep breaths and tried to clear my watering eyes, then I held my breath and returned to the task at hand.

First I emptied the drawer at the bottom of the toilet that was piled high with malodorous turds, befouled tundra, and contraband urine. I then repeatedly hosed off the drum, routinely stopping to empty the catchment tray so that it didn't overflow from the soiled runoff. I cleaned up the mess and got it all reassembled without losing my lunch, but at that point I was one thoroughly disgruntled employee.

I understand that everyone needs to pitch in and get their hands dirty around here for the camp to run smoothly; I have no problem with that. But what I went through today shouldn't be a part of anyone's job description. The composting toilet is a resounding failure and needs to be burned, but the boss refuses to accept defeat and today I had to pay the price for his stubbornness. A price paid in poop.

SEPTEMBER 6

GUILTY PLEASURE

The past two days I have gone downriver with groups of four anglers to harass the silvers that are rapidly approaching their spawn. For these trips we use the larger boats, the twenty-two-foot aluminum v-hulls with 350 Chevy inboards. Just to remain on plane these crafts have to be traveling a minimum of 30 mph, and it isn't difficult to push them over 40. Running at that speed is no big deal when you have rubber tires gripping asphalt, but it gets a little hairy when you're skimming rudderless down a seven-knot current, dodging boulders and whipping around S-turns. The water is very low now, and the potential for boat smashing is high. Our once deep and wide line of travel has diminished to a narrow trickle with little margin for error.

I have a confession to make: I really enjoy running these boats in the river. I know that this can't be good for the ecosystem. As I mentioned before, at the very minimum we're contributing to the erosion of the banks and maybe a great deal more.

I despise certain forms of motor-driven pleasure. I severely dislike NASCAR and I rail against snowmobiling in Yellowstone National Park. Yet here I am, driving these metal beasts which are significantly louder than snowmobiles through a different national park and enjoying every minute of it.

But this is how I make my living. That's the justification with which I attempt to soothe my mental turmoil. I'm a fishing guide who needs these boats to transport my clients. There are a great many people who make their living guiding snowmobile tours through Yellowstone and I don't agree with their method of monetary gain. So how can I justify my own activities? Because I'm guiding fishermen? It just doesn't hold up.

The fact remains: I love the white-knuckle boat trips through the braids. I love the challenge of reading the river and reacting to the sliding chaos of the boat. But if I think about it too much, it really bothers my snooty sense of eco-friendly morality.

SEPTEMBER 7

WE'RE SCREWED

Unlike some fisheries in this area, ours does not fish well into September—especially in odd-numbered years when the pink salmon don't run. Our fishing has come to a screeching halt in the past few days. Every day we have to run farther and farther away to find fish. We didn't hook up with any type of consistency today until we were about twelve miles from camp. That means we floated for twelve miles hooking maybe a half-dozen rainbows between two anglers. After that we got into a few nice fish, and the day was saved, but the line where the fish are holding and feeding continues to sneak farther downstream. How far will we have to go to find them next week? Will we find them at all?

And why did I float through so much water today rather than just driving down? Because my assigned beat was the first four miles of those twelve. I chose to keep going, breaking into other people's water rather than forcing my sports (and myself) to be miserable for an entire day.

It's one thing for people to have slow days when they hire a local guide on their home river; it's quite another when they're dropping many thousands of dollars to be here. An entire week of slow fishing? You can imagine how pleasant an entitled client might be when he has just spent five grand to not catch fish.

The prospect of this was so intimidating that Ken tried to contact all the clients lined up for next week with an offer to roll their deposits over to next season. I admire him for that; it's something not many lodge owners would do. Unfortunately, many of those clients are already in Anchorage.

I have a sinking feeling that our last week will be our most unpleasant. There are a lot of things we can do, but making fish magically appear isn't one of them.

As Dick likes to say, "It's guide . . . not God."

SEPTEMBER 12

INVASION OF THE PINNER

Okay, I really don't want to complain. Though I have had my moments of rapturous elation and crushing frustration these past months, I have loved more than loathed my days on this river.

The final week, however, seems hell-bent on leaving a bad taste in my mouth. It's like waking up after a hard night of drinking. The vague memories of dancing on tables and making out with random women remind me that I've had some serious fun, but it tastes as if someone's cat crapped in my mouth while I snored. That's what this last week is looking like. The party is pretty much over; we're into the cat-crap hangover stage now.

The trout fishing near us has disappeared. In order to get into any fish at all we have to drive ten miles downstream. From there we have a five-mile window where the decaying remains of salmon have created the beautiful from the foul. Bloated rainbows are sulking in the deep runs, and if you can find them they're willing to eat a well-presented flesh pattern. A twenty-inch fish weighs close to four pounds; a twenty-five-incher is much bigger. These bulbous, scaly footballs put on one hell of a show when hooked, but they often find the numerous brush piles in their holes and use them as a means of regaining freedom. If you do manage to land one, they'll often cough up many ounces of decayed, half-digested salmon flesh. It's not a pretty sight.

We have six boats that are competing for the scattered pockets of washed-up death in the five miles of productive river. There's also a fly-out lodge sending four boats into the same water everyday. Plain and simple, we're commuting up to five hours a day roundtrip to not catch many fish. The boats, like the guides, are tired from four straight months of abuse. Mine has broken down every day this week. I've been able to get it going again, but there's nothing that caps off a rough day of fishing like your motor crapping out on the way home—in the rain.

To round out the misery of the final week, I am guiding the most high-maintenance client we've had all season. I took him out last year and he was a handful then, when the fishing was excellent and he was the only sport in camp. With a camp full of clients and horrible fishing, he's . . . well, nearly intolerable.

Adding to his charm is the fact that he practices a style of fishing that I absolutely despise: centerpinning, also known as float fishing. In his mind he has "transcended" fly fishing; he's gotten so good at it that he can no longer find a challenge so he needs something new. Apparently he also fancies himself as an adept steelheader because he further justifies his hobby by proclaiming, "I like to catch steelhead rather than just fish for them."

Both years he has referred to himself as a "one-per-center." He explained to me, in his most condescending tone, that several guides had told him he was in the elite class of people who can actually fish—the top one percent of all anglers. Apparently it's a commonly used phrase, though I had never heard it before. I guess I'm just out of the loop on terminology describing holier-than-thou fly fishermen turned centerpinners. Dammit.

Centerpinning involves a very long rod (thirteen to fourteen feet) and a reel spooled with huge amounts of thin mono-filament. The reel has a free-spinning spool; there is no drag when the line goes out and no clicker as you reel line in. The line, after it exits the rod, has a stout and brightly painted balsa wood bobber followed by a series of small split shot arranged in different patterns to achieve different depths. At the very end is the bait—or in this case, the fly. To use this contraption, the pinner flings his rig into the current and holds his rod aloft while the force of the river pulls line smoothly and consistently off the spinning spool. The result is a near-perfect dead drift that extends as far as one's ability to see the bright orange bobber.

I know nothing about pinning. I've never done it—don't have any desire to do it. From what I understand it's a very effective method for presenting a fly (or bait) to fish. Despite my lack of experience with this fishing style, he wants me on his hip constantly consulting as he moves his "shot pattern" a quarter inch this way and an eighth inch that way so that his bobber will "set up" properly. If this were earlier in the season, I would stand a better chance at feigning interest, but at this point I just can't get there. At least that's how it feels to me. It seems, however, that I've done a sufficiently good job at pretending to care because he's requested me all week.

The person that I feel for most in this situation is the perfectly nice, easygoing fly fisherman who got partnered up with the Pinner for the week. They are the only two singles in camp, so they're stuck together as boat mates for the duration.

Here's an example of what the fly caster and I have been dealing with for the past few days. Yesterday we were drift-fishing flesh flies under indicators. The Pinner will use his fly rod for this purpose, but he isn't happy about it. His prized "float rod" was lying in the boat with about two feet of the tip hanging off the stern as we drifted. The Pinner was in the bow and the fly guy was in the stern. The fly guy hooked a snag, and his line caught the overhanging tip of the Pinner's float rod as we drifted past the spot where he was hung up. The fly guy was aware of the situation and was making every effort to ensure that his line didn't exert too much pressure on the float rod and cause the tip to snap. As soon as the tip of his rod bent slightly against the tightening fly line, the Pinner begins SCREAMING at the top of his lungs like a ten-year-old girl.

"NO, NO, NO, NO, NOOOOOOOO!"

Remember, this is a grown man.

The fly guy successfully angled his rod to snap the line without damaging the Pinner's float rod. He then turned to the asshole and spoke in a voice that one would use when addressing a child in mid-tantrum. "Calm down. Screaming will not accomplish anything."

I sat between them on the sticks, pretending to cough into my jacket and hoping the laughter wasn't too obvious.

Three more days.

SEPTEMBER 13

THE DANCE OF DECOMPOSITION, A.K.A. THE SKANKY SALMON SHUFFLE

Fall snuck up behind me. One day I woke up and it was dark. Except for a few groggy midnight moments, I hadn't seen dark in months. Now all of a sudden I need to dig out my thoroughly buried head-lamp to relieve myself during the night. Well, not really. I just step outside my front door and let fly. It's nice to have a reading light, though.

Today as we planed toward a particularly pungent grav-el bar, I noticed that yellow and orange has seeped into the river-bank foliage. The scattered birch trees are blazing and the stalks of sinewy grass that line the banks have all gone to a purplish brown seed. The wind has cut its fall teeth, and this morning it gnawed through the residual moisture in the cuffs of my jacket. The season is ending; it's really ending. Despite my cerebral knowledge of this fact, I required these visual cues to ignite my visceral belief.

I got a reprieve from Pinner duty today and guided some decent fishermen whom I actually wanted to catch fish. We were assigned a beat that hasn't been fishing very well, but I was determined to produce for my clients. My mojo has been wind-knot-ted this week, and it was time to detangle.

After the frigid haul downriver we pulled up to a wide flat, striated with gravel bars and dotted with islands. I knew that many chums had spawned and died in the braids directly above this spot, so I figured I could find some pockets of rot and trout nearby. I managed to find a nice pile of salmon corpses, but after a few drifts we hadn't had a single pull. At that point I decided to shuck my morals and get dirty.

Just up from my clients, I stepped into a back eddy packed with rotten, submerged salmon and danced a jig. I got after it. Picture a gangly, bearded white guy wearing waders in waist-deep water trying out for Soul Train. That was me. I slipped and slid and stepped and spun until a slick of opaque, foul-smelling rot billowed downcurrent below me. Oddly enough, one of my guys hooked up on the next cast. This is something I've never done before. I am not a fan of chumming tactics like the San Juan Shuffle, and I've been known to give people on the river a piece of my mind when I see them doing the Gravel Bar Dance and stirring up salmon eggs into the current. But desperate times require desperate measures, dammit, and I was pretty sick of not catching fish.

I'm not going to say that my rotten white-boy funk moves created a banner day, but it was a vast improvement over the past few. We caught about twenty-five rainbows, most of them over twenty inches.

I felt a little dirty when I got back to camp. Partially because my wading boots have a new odor emanating from their felt soles and partially because I feel like I cheated a little—like I cut a corner. Shit, it's better than coating my flesh flies in WD-40, and I know a few guides up here who've done that.

The motto around this camp is: "Do what you have to do to catch fish." I've always prided myself on not needing to resort to questionable tactics, but today I drove the lower road. After the misery of yesterday's five fish (yes, five!) it was worth it to maintain my sanity.

SEPTEMBER 14

A CHANGE OF PACE

One of the sports this week has been wanting to do some pike fishing. He's a fly shop owner from Virginia who's a lot of fun to have in the boat. So far he hasn't been able to talk anyone into hiking to the pike lake, but today he was successful—and surprisingly it was Mr. Pinner. Obviously, he can't use the centerpinning technique in still water, so he brought along his fly rod instead. He's an accomplished fly caster but not nearly as good as he thinks he is.

What this meant for me was a much-needed departure from the long, downriver commute and the grindingly slow trout fishing. So today I got to hike to one of my favorite pieces of water and watch these unlikely companions tromp around with bent rods like goofy teenagers. I just set them up and let them go. I didn't have to focus myself into a stress headache because I couldn't figure out the trout and I wasn't meeting expectations. All they had to do was step into the lake, cast around the reeds, and WHAM! That's all there was to it.

I waded between them unhooking fish and taking pictures. I sat on a rock and contemplated the view that stretched out before me. I spent twenty minutes picking wild blueberries and stuffing them into my mouth.

I was nervous about how it would go with Mr. Pinner. The fly shop owner kind of talked him into the pike fishing, and the Pinner is pretty anal about his trout. A successful real estate developer from Florida, he's wound so tight that he vibrates on a frequency only dogs can hear. I didn't think he'd be able to let go and enjoy something different. I was wrong.

The two of them hopped from one weed patch to the next, giggling, comparing fish, and cheering each other on. I have no idea how many pike they caught, but it was a lot. The fly shop owner had one snap his rod tip, but he laughed it off. He broke off a few extra inches and still managed to cast forty feet without the top two guides.

They wanted to take a couple of fish back to camp for hors d' oeuvres, and that's when I learned how difficult it is to kill a pike. I bonked one of them over the head twice, sliced all his gills, and dropped him belly up in a pool to keep the meat fresh until we were ready to go home. Four hours later we came back and he was gone! After a few minutes of poking around the area I found him lying in the weeds, flaring his gills. He wasn't in good shape, but he wasn't dead. No wonder pike have survived since prehistory and populated multiple continents.

I needed this day. It was a perfect recharge for tomorrow—the last day. I want to end on a high note and now I feel like I can get after them. Trout beware, I'm coming for you.

Oh yeah, just to top off a good day, we stopped at one hole on the way back and hooked ten silvers in half an hour.

SEPTEMBER 15

THE LAST DAY

I awoke this morning just a few seconds before my alarm rang. My sleep and work cycles have become deeply entrenched. It was still dark outside my tent, cold and crisp. My steps were springy as I bounced down the hill to the final breakfast. The impending sunrise spread faint orange tendrils of light above the horizon, and a dense fog blanketed the river.

Pancakes. How fitting.

I doubt that I'll ever order pancakes again. I used to like them as an occasional breakfast treat. Now, after months of eating them once, sometimes twice a week, I have lost my taste for them completely. The problem with pancakes is that I eat them with syrup. The combination of the simple carbohydrates and pure sugar first thing in the morning causes a spike in my blood sugar and sets me up for a mid-morning crash. I've come to dread pancake day almost as much as powdered-biscuits-and-canned-gravy day.

My fingers froze numb on the tiller handle as we ran downriver in search of trout. It was difficult to concentrate on the route. My head was on a swivel and my eyes were darting about like a juvenile brown bear, aimlessly trying to take it all in at once. I had to make a few last-second swerves around rocks that I had avoided countless times previously.

We went back to the original arrangement today: myself, the Pinner, and the same fly guy that fished with us before. Today, though, neither the Pinner's high-voltage expectations nor the palpable tension between him and the fly guy could penetrate my armor of optimism.

The last day. My knowledge that it would all end this afternoon allowed me a detached perspective from which to observe. Without the stress of additional guiding days looming on the calendar, I was able to appreciate the amusing situation that these two clashing personae created when forced to fish together. Today, without the pressure that I've felt for the past week, I found myself intrigued with the Pinner's general twitchiness and bizarre behavior.

We fished from the boat for a great deal of the day. We were searching for active trout and eventually found them sitting behind the scattered silvers that had finally paired up and begun to spawn. I walked the boat along, holding it from the bow, with the Pinner up near me and the fly guy fishing from the stern. I had them both using fly rods with beads that closely matched the salmon spawn.

The Pinner would make extremely animated casting motions, and when fighting a fish he looked like some kind of dancer. He called it "the choreography of his fishing ballet." His other annoying habit was to cast perpendicular to the boat and selfishly extend his drifts as far as he possibly could. This would force the fly guy to hold his rod tip out away from the boat and postpone his next cast. This went on for about an hour before the fly guy got fed up and started casting whenever he felt like it. This, of course, led to monstrous tangles, which in turn caused the high-strung Pinner to become impatient and angry.

When we stopped a bit later to fish a hole for trout, the Pinner pulled me aside and whispered, "I'm amazed at your level of patience with such inept angling; doesn't that just drive you nuts? It's obvious that he has no concept of how to fish from a boat. Isn't there anything you can do?"

I laughed and replied, "I'm accustomed to much worse." And then I walked away.

The show that the Pinner put on today was like nothing I've ever seen. This is the kind of self-absorbed character that you simply cannot invent. At one point this morning he hooked a very nice trout and lost it after a minute or two. I walked up behind him just as the line went slack and listened to him chide himself mercilessly. "That was a MASSIVE fish; that was a big fish. I can't BELIEVE I lost that fish. That was the fish of the trip and I lost him, I just lost him. Oh my God. Oh God. That was a huge trout. That fish was a major player."

A major player? Who the hell refers to a trout as a "major player"?

Later that day he landed his biggest fish of the trip, a beautiful rainbow of about seven or eight pounds. He jumped up in the air and pumped his fist screaming to the sky, "I LOVE THIS!" I could only wonder whom he was trying to convince. Was it me? himself? the river? As we were taking pictures, he made me switch hats with him. He wanted to be wearing one of our lodge hats so that he would have a chance to be on the cover of next year's brochure.

At the end of the day the fly guy and I were ready to go home, but I practically had to drag the Pinner back to the boat. I explained to him that it was quitting time and reminded him that all the other lodge boats had already gone past. He spent the ride home yelling over the engine and trying to convince me to take him out the next morning to fish the hour between breakfast and when his plane arrived. I pretended I couldn't hear him and lost myself in the colors of changing foliage that smeared my peripheral vision.

After dropping off my two clients at the dock, I pulled into the boat slough for the last time. The other guides were all there, hugging, high-fiving, and exchanging weary grins. We worked until dinner pulling boats up on shore, winterizing motors, and setting ourselves up for an easy transition next spring. My waders had made it through the whole season with minimal trauma, but on the last day they blew out. My left leg was saturated when I finally squished up the hill and peeled away the layers.

It's time to go home.

SEPTEMBER 16—20

THE JOURNEY HOME

I startled awake this morning to a bright, humid dawn, totally unsure of where I was. I knew that I was no longer in camp. The bed was too soft, I didn't smell dog and wet waders, and I was lying under clean sheets, not cocooned in a filmy sleeping bag.

For a moment I thought I was still in Seattle, but it felt too warm. As consciousness seeped into my mind, I soaked up the realization that I had made it back home. My childhood room in my parent's house in Hawaii. I haven't lived here in a decade, but I still think of it as home.

I rolled over and looked at the clock. It was 6:00 a.m. I wished I could have slept more, but my internal clock was still running on Alaska time. I lay there for a while and recounted my travels of the past few days. It felt good to lie in a real bed without anyone waiting for me to be awake, perky, and knowledgeable.

The clenching tension of all that happened between leaving camp and arriving here is slowly dissipating. I feel sore all over, but the muscles in my jaw are particularly tight. I haven't touched my laptop in nearly a week. Noisy, crowded airports are one of my favorite places to write, but this time I lacked the energy. Besides, it felt preemptive to write it all down before I had reached my final destination.

Sunday

I awoke early, ate quickly, and set about the task of organizing all my belongings into fish boxes and dry bags. More than anything, I wanted to avoid the Pinner and his begging me to take him fishing. I was done guiding.

I made haphazard stacks on the plywood floor of clothes, fishing gear, and electronics that would be stuffed into various waterproof duffels and carried across oceans. Toiletries and excess gear were piled into waxed cardboard boxes and duct-taped shut. They would be stored in the crawl space above the bathrooms to freeze solid over the long winter.

As I packed and organized, I could hear faint rumblings of commotion from the dock, the sounds of the last clients leaving. For the past seventeen weeks I've been a part of that process of carrying luggage, firm handshakes, empty future fishing promises, and either standing on the dock smiling and waving or getting behind the wheel of the boat and navigating everyone safely downstream. On that final Sunday, I did neither; I sat in my tent, alone, and packed. I was no longer on call. I didn't have to force a smile or pretend to like anyone; I just went about the task of packing away a temporary life.

When the final boat returned from depositing our last group of clients into their floatplanes, a massive cheer went through the camp. I heard our head guide running between the Weatherports screaming, "They're gone! They're gone! HA HA, they're fucking gone! I can say FUCK all I want to. I can say FUCK and scream and yell and do whatever the FUCK I want because they're FUCKING GONE!"

At 3:00 p.m. the Weatherports were down and our boat was loaded for departure. We all migrated to the dining room to eat cheeseburgers and bask in the easy laughter that had eluded our tight group for months. Dillis and Paul and I were going out on the evening high tide; everyone else was staying around for a few more days to break down camp and shoot ducks.

When Paul selflessly designated himself the responsible driver, Dillis and I responded with our natural inclination: we started drinking. At 4:00 p.m. we were loaded into one of the twenty-two-foot single inboard 350s. We had the three of us, two dogs, all of our gear, a twelve-pack, a half bag of trail mix, a quart of water, six duck meat empanadas, and enough cathartic excitement to howl as we roared away from the dock with our compatriots waving, laughing, and flipping us off.

We hit the mouth of the river on the waxing tide. There was enough water to get out, but just barely. We skipped over one mudflat so shallow the boat didn't even leave a wake, just a brown, muddy churn extending behind us. Dillis and I were deep into the twelve-pack as we entered the bay and began skirting the emergent mudflats. Dillis stood on the engine cowling, yelling and riding the rise and fall of the open ocean waves. I stuck my head out the side window and let the salt spray assail my face and beard as our bow crashed over three-foot rollers. Paul did an expert job managing the narrow channels and rolling swells. Our smiles could not be contained. We were home free.

A desolate peninsula crowned with the burned-out shell of a long dead cannery marks the halfway point of the bay crossing. At that point I needed to relieve myself, so I stood and made my way to the stern on wobbly legs. I unhitched my leaky waders and pressed one knee against the cowling and the other against the gunnel to support myself as recycled beer trickled off the stern. As I stared into our muddy wake, feeling total relief wash over my body . . . the engine seized up. It didn't sputter or cough; it just died—with utter and complete finality.

"THE PLUG! PUT IN THE PLUG!" Paul screamed as he tried in vain to get the engine started again. We had been running with the drain plug out because the boat had sustained pretty serious damage to the hull earlier in the season. Running with the plug out allowed the water we were taking in through the cracked hull to drain out on its own. With my waders still unattached, I threw open the cowling and stopped the flow of seawater that was filling our engine box. After three tries the starter wouldn't even grind anymore and we had to make some quick decisions. We were completely at the mercy of Bristol Bay, a cold and expansive body of water that's not known for its leniency. Luckily for us, however, the wind was blowing onshore and the tide was still coming in. With the aid of those forces we were able to paddle and kedge our way to shore. Had the tide been going out or the wind pushing the opposite direction, we would have simply drifted out to sea in a sinking boat.

As it was, we were not set adrift—we were simply stranded, stranded on a muddy flat on the edge of Bristol Bay twenty miles from our destination. We worked for a couple of hours trying to figure out what was wrong with the engine. There was no progress. We had no radio and no satellite phone and darkness was approaching. My burgeoning beer buzz evaporated with the realization that we weren't going to make it to town that night and our chances of catching our 11:00 a.m. flight in the morning were akin to the dogs sprouting wings and flying us out themselves.

Our spirits were crushed. Dillis and I lay in the tall grass on the shoreline, stared at the scuttling clouds, and tried not to talk about our misfortune. Our dogs curled up beside us, totally drained from all of the panic and yelling. We were lucky, really lucky. We were thin on food and water, but there was no real or immediate threat to our safety. Someone would come looking for us, though probably not before nightfall. The only thing we could do was wait. Every few minutes one of us would break the silence by yelling, "Goddammit, we should be in the bar right now!"

The leak in my waders proved to be ill-timed after all. We had jumped into the water to secure the boat, and my left leg was soaked to the skin. The thought of a soggy, shivering night on the edge of Bristol Bay put me in a foul mood, and I got into a yelling argument with Paul over how to deal with the leaking boat. I stormed off like a spurned child and wandered the marshy grasslands near the edge of the bay until I calmed down. It was all coming to a head, a whole season of frustration bottled into this one moment. Now, when I should have been basking in my accom-plishment and enjoying a hard-earned rest, I was instead furious and freezing and preparing to spend a miserable night on a bar-ren shoreline. I walked and fumed until the acute sharpness of total disappointment had ebbed into a dull, constant ache. I then returned, apologized, and helped them get the boat squared away.

We decided to walk it slowly offshore as the tide ebbed and anchor it where it would eventually go dry during the night's low tide. In that position the boat couldn't take on water and sink, but we also had to make sure that it was far enough from shore so the morning (smaller) high tide could float it. We jockeyed it into position until well after dark. Around 11:00 p.m. our ailing vessel finally settled into the mud.

Paul slept in the boat while Dillis and I shared his one-man pup tent. The grassy point of land where we stopped was not the greatest campsite. The ground was pocked with craters, but at least it was somewhat soft. We stole a couple of hours of sleep from the cold, damp night.

Monday

We awoke at sunrise, pulled on our waders, and waited for the incoming tide to float our boat. We ate handfuls of trail mix and our duck meat empanadas for breakfast. Paul wished for coffee and I wished for a plane; we broke into impulsive, weary laughter. After that there was nothing to do but wait.

We finally spotted our rescuers out in the bay at 10:45—fifteen minutes before our flight was scheduled to leave King Salmon. We held up a blue tarp in the wind to catch their attention and watched as they changed their heading and bounced toward us through the surf. Dick and Josh have never looked so attractive; I could have kissed them, but I think that would have been awkward.

By the time we towed the boat to the dock, trailered both of them, unloaded our gear, and drove to the airport, it was 2:15 p.m. Our boss, knowing we wouldn't make our flights, had called the airline and rebooked us on the only remaining seats that day. Paul and I were leaving King Salmon at 3:00, and Dillis and the dogs were leaving at 5:00. Paul and I hurriedly gathered our gear and promised to meet Dillis at the Anchorage airport when he got in. There was no time to eat or change clothes. We pulled off our wet, muddy waders, stuffed them in our duffels, and boarded our flight.

In Anchorage Paul and I stepped off the plane and into the humming throng of humanity and machinery that accompanies a major metropolitan airport. After four months in the bush it was a bit of a shock. I was too tired to do anything but follow the checklist in my head: find baggage claim, avoid crowd of hugging Midwesterners, put bags on cart, find airport shuttle, check into Holiday Inn, find room, drop baggage.

Lisa was there waiting for us. She had come to town the day before we had and was the one who sounded the alarm when our boat never arrived at the dock in King Salmon. She met us with huge hugs and tears brimming.

"Holy shit, I thought you guys were lost. I'm so happy to see you."

It was one of the best hugs ever.

I wanted to collapse on the bed, but I knew if I did, I'd be done for the night. Instead I got back in the airport shuttle and went back to pick up Dillis and the dogs. When I arrived at the airport, I saw that his flight had been delayed for two hours. For the third time in just over an hour, I got back in the Holiday Inn airport shuttle. The driver, Maurice, was a polite and well-groomed black man who seemed distinctly out of place in the great white north. We were now on a first-name basis. We laughed at my situation, and he suggested that I'd probably feel better if I showered and shaved and put on some decent clothes. I was too tired to explain that I didn't own any decent clothes. I just nodded in agreement.

Back at the hotel, Paul was arguing with the phone company and trying to get his cell phone turned back on while I stared at Sports Center, attempting to catch up on the new football season. My eyelids began to droop as soon as I reclined, so I decided to go for a walk instead. The gritty air of downtown Anchorage irritated my eyes and lungs, and I had trouble gauging the distance and speed of traffic as I crossed roads. I wandered aimlessly looking for a sandwich shop and a liquor store. I hadn't eaten in nearly twenty-four hours and was in dire need of a beer. I stopped random people on the street to ask where I could find these items. They seemed caught off guard by a stranger interrupting their private urban bubbles. They gave me curious, standoffish looks but also gave me directions. After an hour of wandering the streets I was beginning to adjust to the sounds of car horns and the feel of concrete under my shoes. I made it back to the hotel room with snacks and a twelve-pack of beer—in bottles!

We both took showers and felt slightly rejuvenated as we climbed back into Maurice's van and returned, yet again, to the airport. We walked into the terminal to check the electronic signage that was supposed to direct us to our friend's flight. Flight 1247 from King Salmon had disappeared from the boards. It was gone; like it had fallen into the Alaska Triangle. It took three different gate agents to even validate that such a flight had ever existed. The clerk informed me that the plane had had "mechanical difficulties," the exact nature of which she did not know. The plane was stuck in Dillingham (an armpit not unlike King Salmon) and would not arrive until 1:00 a.m. at the earliest.

Exhausted, hungry, and without any recourse to find my friend or my dog, I did what any rational human being would do at that point, I went in search of more food and alcohol. Paul, Lisa, and I ate a much-appreciated dinner at Humpie's, had more than a couple of drinks, and promptly caught a cab to Anchorage's famous strip joint, the The Great Alaskan Bush Company.

I don't like strip clubs, never have. I look around at all the men slobbering on themselves as they watch women undress— women who mostly despise them. Then it occurs to me that I'm one of them and I become depressed. It sort of kills the strip club mood. For some reason, though, this feeling was minimized by the fact that we went there at the insistence of a woman. Lisa fed us a consistent barrage of shots, and I was just beginning to get comfortable when she dragged Paul and me by the hands up to the meat rack where men sit with necks craned like giraffes as the dancers undulate with spread legs.

Lisa insisted that we each get lap dances, so she began appraising the various working women until she found one she liked. She did this under the guise of finding a hot girl to dance for us, but she was really looking for the one that appealed to her. She finally found one she liked, and Paul and I slurped our drinks and flashed each other nervous, adolescent grins as we watched Lisa lose herself in a moment of inebriated arousal. I must admit, Jasmine did have a talent for working her body and our wallets.

At 1:15 a.m. we dragged each other out of the Bush Company and hopped a cab to the airport. The driver was gaunt and ghostly pale, like a vampire. He wore a leather cowboy hat and a long ponytail. A bleached whalebone cross hung from his rearview mirror.

I slurred at him, "We gotta pick up our friend from the airport, that's why we gotta take this goddamn cab."

He held my gaze for a moment with washed-out eyes and then held a finger up to the cross. "This is a god-blessed cab," he said. His tone was direct and emotionless, his cheek bones pushed out at his limp flesh.

"Oh yeah, cool. Let's go." I didn't say another word to him. I wished I were sitting in the back and giggling in hushed tones with Paul and Lisa. He me made me very uneasy.

Of the three of us Paul was the least drunk, or at least the best at handling his intoxication. At the airport he took over the duty of trying to figure out what happened to Dillis's plane while Lisa and I ran around the terminal looking for an open bar and yelling like a couple of drunken monkeys. I vaguely remember throwing her over my shoulder and riding the elevator up and down repeatedly, asking strangers if they knew where we could get some drinks. When we were satisfied that there really was nothing open, we fell into a row of seats to wait. I was utterly depleted and couldn't keep my eyes focused. Exhaustion and alcohol are a poor mix. I felt a deep empathy for Dillis as I sat there waiting for his flight. We had been planning this blowout in Anchorage for months. It was fun, but it wasn't the same without him.

Dillis and the dogs finally arrived in Anchorage at 2:30 a.m. After their flight left King Salmon the pilots apparently realized that the landing gear was broken. For reasons no one could grasp, they decided to bring it down in Dillingham rather than Anchorage, where there would be more emergency support. So instead of heading toward their original destination, they crash-landed at the ill-equipped Dillingham airport and waited there for six hours while another plane was brought in.

Our buddy, Maurice, picked up our bedraggled group around 3:00 a.m., and we staggered into the hotel to catch a few hours of fitful sleep.

Tuesday
Dillis, the dogs, and I were scheduled to fly out early in the afternoon. The dogs still needed their vet certificates for transport, and since I wasn't involved in the plane crash in Dillingham, I volunteered to get up early and deal with the animals. When I woke, I could feel small men with hammers working at the insides of my temples and my stomach rumbled with residual whiskey. At 8:00 a.m. I forced myself out of bed and began scouring the Yellow Pages for a vet who could take us in that morning.

The vet certification went smoothly, and we made it to the airport in time to catch our flights. We bid Paul and Lisa a heartfelt good-bye at the hotel. Dillis and I parted ways at the airport with a succinct, masculine hug. He was kind enough to take my dog all the way back to Montana with him while I skipped off for a couple weeks of vacation.

I spent Tuesday night in Seattle with a friend from college and jumped an early flight the next day to Hawaii. My father was waiting for me at the curb wearing a subdued smile and holding a flower lei.

Thursday

Here I am in the bedroom where I spent my childhood, listening to the trade winds frolic in the wind chimes and thinking about the whirlwind of the past few days and the season that preceded them. It's early yet, and no one else is awake. These are the first moments I've had to reflect on the trip home and sketch out some thoughts.

Most likely I'll go back for another summer. I waded through my share of muddy frustration this year. I felt the weight and grip of it pulling at my feet, but it never dragged me down completely.

There are a few things that will keep me tied to that place, to that river. In general, I enjoy guiding and I feel that I'm pretty good at it. I enjoy the thrill of others catching fish. Guiding is similar to fishing but more difficult. Even though you may know how to catch the fish, you still have to coax someone through the process who may have less ability. You have to coach the right cast, the appropriate presentation, a timely hook-set, and an effective fight.

Guiding, for me, is not about barking orders and putting people on edge. I prefer a gentle lead that keeps the client engaged and allows me to experiment and try new things throughout the day. I can get away with only so many failed experiments before my client begins to lose faith in my advice. Once they've lost faith, the day (possibly the week) is pretty well shot. Such challenges keep me interested, though occasionally they are overwhelming. I'm a better guide in June than September.

Another reason I'll go back is for the people, the core staff that we have in camp. People like Dan come and go. He went pretty quickly, by the way—right after the spike camp snafu. The boss gets some bad hires from year to year, but our returning core is solid. We're a tight-knit group of extremely disparate individuals. We have a southern good-ole-boy duck hunter, a commercial fisherman, a master electrician, and an extreme-sports cameraman. We hail from North Carolina to Hawaii.

When I arrived my first year, I couldn't see how I would possibly mesh within such a diverse group. I vowed to keep my head down, my mouth shut, and get through it. Over the months our sweat soaking into the frozen mud became our commonality. We erected bridges of friendship with dirty dishwater, engine grease, and deck screws. Our opinions on culture, religion, media, and social issues might have clashed and produced a tumultuous confrontation anywhere else, but in Alaska they were unimportant. We trusted each other; we placed our lives and well-being in each other's hands. That loyalty alone prevented any lasting conflict among us. The collective smiles, grimaces, yells, and laughter that reflected off that river bonded into a connection that transcended our backgrounds. I may not see or speak to the majority of the people I left standing on that dock until next May, but our understanding and faith in one another will remain unchanged until next season.

The river and the ecosystem also have a part in the bond that I feel for this job. Though it makes it difficult to have a normal life, healthy relationships, and a stable income, I am not yet ready to let it go. There's something about the harsh beauty of that place that has captured my soul. I arrive each season with soft, clean hands and depart with calloused palms, split knuckles, missing fingernails, and cracked, stained flesh. The frigid waters of the river inundate me and strip away the layers. At the end of the season I am left raw and pulsing. I am not diminished by this loss; I am fortified by it. Like a molting, I have shed a skin weighted with history, a skin permeated with doubt and fear, and I'm left fresh with confidence and the knowledge that I can survive, even flourish, in an environment that is abrasive and unforgiving.

With the dawn creeping into view from this slatted window and this soft bed, I will rise before anyone else. I will put on my shoes and run a few miles on the beach. I'll find the rhythm of my breath and match it to the warm ocean surf that I've known since I was a kid. I'll run until my legs burn and my chest heaves and then I'll kick off my shoes, dive into the water, and swim through the wind-chopped beach break. The water will cradle me. It will hold me afloat and slowly soak into my ravaged hands. In a few days, they will start to heal.

RANDOM COMMENTARY FROM THE MESSAGE BOARD AT DRAKEMAG.COM

Just what I needed on yet another Monday morning in my paper-stacked hole. Thanks for making it a little better. —VIKING

Gaper, damned nice read. Now get back to work. —ADAMS

At least you're not on one of those crab boats. —FLIESONLY

I smell a book in the making. —2HI2FISH

Not to be too much of an ingrate, Gaper, but I don't think we're getting the full flavor of the town bar. —SNAGLY

This is The Drake's version of Penthouse Letters. —SURLY

I'm most impressed with the Internet system that is available to you in that part of the country. Are you using aluminum foil?
                                                    —KROMAGNUM

Of course this could all be staged in his backyard, kind of like the moon landing, you know. —STATUTORY RAP

It's funny how after spending many hours on the water up there guiding many different types of people, the ones who are the most appreciative of the entire experience and just happy to be there are often rewarded. It's as if the waters seem to respond in a different way to people who are unpretentious. Amazing! —WRH

Gaper, send an order to town for one of the two-pound packs of unscented Handi Wipes. Cleans what's necessary, let the rest get shiny. —GEEZER

I love how the writing has gotten progressively more refined since the fishing started. —COOLCONMAN

*G*aper, when you work in an office, there is no "twenty-three-incher that took a caddis on the last cast saved my day." Just a computer, phone, shitty cup of coffee, and some tech support feller telling you to do exactly as you thought he would: reboot the sonofabitch. Be glad for the rain, the bears, the soggy shithouse, and most importantly the river that serves as your commute to work everyday.
—CREEKLOVER

*I*t feels like I'm watching instead of reading these reports.
—GOFISHER

*Y*ou guys know, don't you, that Gaper is really just an overweight 50-year-old hermaphrodite living in his deceased grandmother's basement, masturbating all day to gay porn and burning his arms at night because his Mormon upbringing has polluted his mind beyond rectification. He's been searching for stock photos of Alaska and posting them here just to string you guys along. —BURBOT

*Y*ou let him use your net? —BADNOTS

*I'*m gonna forward this thread to my mom. —FATBACK

*M*y three favorite fishing books: The Longest Silence, Thomas Mc-Guane; A River Runs Through It, Norman Maclean; The AK Chronicles, Gaper. —BRUISER

*B*eware Ebay shoppers for a Simms jacket and waders "barely used" for sale in the near future. —WRH

*M*adness! MADNESS! —BROOKWOOKIE

A quick Google search of lower back stretches should point you in the right direction. Just don't do some of those stretches in public or you might get some new friends around camp. —STEELHYDE

Two Vicodin and two beers every six hours and you'll be fine.
—HIGHSTREAM

We are in the presence of greatness. A master is among us. My dreams aren't this good. —FLYMPH

Those white-collar millionaire guys have the same problems you blue-collar guys do: divorce, broken cars, leaky roofs, but their problems are much bigger and more expensive than yours.
—FLYBUG.PA.

To think that at one point, Gaper suggested this thread might end prematurely. Thank God it didn't. —COLORADICUS

Too bad you can't take a flamethrower to Dan. —SEWER TROUT

Haven't really been on The Drake in a while now, but heard some underground reference to a story about a guy in Alaska—they call it The AK Chronicles. Had to check it out . . . and I'm a better person for having done so. —URSUS

Well done, Gaper. For the last couple of months the first thing I did after work was check for more of your posts. For that, thank you, and I wish you well. Now, go get laid. —FLYBUG.PA.

Thank you, sir, for bringing a measure of joy to this office denizen. I am truly sad to see it end. —FLOODTIDE

I don't know why, but I got a tear rolling down my face. ONLY ONE, THOUGH, BITCHES! —CRICK ADDICT